# All Money Is Not

## Created Equal

# All Money Is Not Created Equal

## How Entrepreneurs Can Crack the Code to Getting the Right Funding for Their Startup

**David Spreng**

WILEY

Published by John Wiley & Sons, Inc., Hoboken, New Jersey.
Published simultaneously in Canada.

For general information on our other products and services or for technical support, please contact our Customer Care Department within the United States at (800) 762-2974, outside the United States at (317) 572-3993 or fax (317) 572-4002.

Wiley also publishes its books in a variety of electronic formats. Some content that appears in print may not be available in electronic formats. For more information about Wiley products, visit our web site at www.wiley.com.

*Library of Congress Cataloging-in-Publication Data is Available:*

ISBN 9781119887805 (Cloth)
ISBN 9781119887829 (ePDF)
ISBN 9781119887812 (ePUB)

Cover Design: Tricia Principe
Cover Images: © Bet_Noire/Getty Images; © bombermoon/Getty Images
Author photo: Courtesy of Runway Growth Capital

SKY10048395_052423

*To all the entrepreneurs dreaming of changing the world, sacrificing so much in the endless pursuit of your noble ambition.*

# Contents

# Foreword

David and I were first introduced more than 10 years ago by Max von Bismarck, who was then the Head of Investors Industry Group for the World Economic Forum (WEF). Max suggested that David and I collaborate in organizing a reception for finance and business leaders during the WEF annual meeting in Davos. Ever since, we've been hosting an annual party that's acquired a reputation for being an event where great wine and even greater ideas flow in abundance. (I'm pretty sure, given the caliber of people who attend the World Economic Forum, the ideas would come anyhow, but the wine sure doesn't hurt.)

On the surface, David and I aren't an obvious pair. David is low-key and understated. He is the kind of whip-smart guy who doesn't need to let you know right away just how smart he is and will slay you with funny stories that you just don't see coming. He is level-headed, even-keeled, and nobody's fool. I like and admire all those things about him.

On the other hand, it would be fair to say that reticence and reserve are not qualities I possess in abundance. If you're looking for proof that opposites attract, come to our next party at Davos.

Deep down, though, what David and I share, in addition to an appreciation of good wine, is an entrepreneurial spirit and a desire to help other companies grow and prosper.

We both started out in investment banking, which gives you a great overview of how companies and fortunes are made (and, yes, often lost). Over the years, we each forged our own paths in the financial world.

David eventually landed in the world of venture debt. In just a few years, his firm, Runway Growth Capital, has acquired a reputation for helping companies grow and increase in value while allowing founders to keep a greater percentage of their equity.

As a guy who has built his own businesses, I know how important it is to be judicious about where your money comes from, under what terms, and at what juncture in your business. And I can definitely appreciate the idea of helping founders hold on to more ownership of the companies they've created.

In this book, David has taken what he has learned as an investment banker, a venture capitalist, and a growth lender to give founders and would-be entrepreneurs a master class in the key things they need to know about funding for startups. I don't know of any other book that touches on so many aspects of funding or does so in a way that is both deft and efficient.

David is ethical, fair, reasonable, and can see beyond the square box that debt is often conscribed to. He is a firm believer that business can – and should – be a win-win proposition. He helps make it that way.

I didn't yet know David when I wrote my book *Goodbye Gordon Gekko: How to Find Your Fortune Without Losing Your Soul,* but I could have been writing about him. In a sense I feel like I did.

He isn't about transactions but partnership, and, if you're really lucky, friendship. I'm one of the lucky ones because I call him my friend.

Anthony Scaramucci
Founder and managing partner of SkyBridge Capital

# Acknowledgments

Any book is an act of co-creation, involving scores of people: the executives and others who gave their time and shared their stories and insights, the friends and family who gave up their time so that I could work on the book, professional colleagues, Bill Falloon and the rest of the publishing team at Wiley that supported, counseled, edited, and challenged me and ultimately brought this book into being, and many more.

I would specifically like to thank my colleagues at Runway Growth Capital for their support and patience while I learned how to research and write a book and Patricia O'Connell, who, as a professional writer, nurtured my learning process at every step and without whom this book would not have materialized.

Finally, and most importantly, I want to thank my family. My wife, Valeryia, and children (Jack, Sarah, Chloe, and Nikita) have been patient and understanding beyond compare. Much of the work for this book took place on weekends, which means it occupied hours that would otherwise have been spent with family and friends. Valeryia endured those absences without complaint. I am eternally grateful for her love, support, and forbearance.

# Introduction

Venture capital (VC) is often seen as the Holy Grail for founders with a big idea for their company. Having a great idea for a business is the start – but it isn't enough. You need capital to bring your idea to fruition. The quest for money to keep a dream – and a business – alive can be as consuming and stressful as the search for the technological breakthrough or market niche that will make a business viable and valuable. As you follow your dream, raising money is like walking a tightrope: one wrong step can be fatal.

Money, like everything else of value, comes at a price. For founders, the price often ends up being too high. In my 30 years of helping companies get the money they need to grow, I've seen too many really smart, hardworking entrepreneurs end up with too little to show for their blood, toil, tears, and sweat. Multiple rounds of equity investment from venture capitalists (VCs) can leave them with ownership stakes diluted to the point where they end up owning just a small fraction of the company they founded.

Reduced ownership stakes mean less profit for founders as well as for early-stage employees who trade low salaries for the promise of small equity stakes. It also means less control – less say in how a company is run, and less voice in its future (which could be an IPO, a sale to a strategic buyer, a merger, an acquisition of another company, or shutting down).

In my experience, the loss of control is often what disappoints and frustrates founders most. Entrepreneurs are driven by more than money; vision and purpose are what propel them to attempt the improbable and to keep going, on a path that is challenging at best.

Entrepreneurs aren't doomed to dilution and disappointment. There is more than one way to finance growth – and that's what I mean when I say, "all money is not created equal."

The disparity in what different forms of financing can mean has profound implications for founders. Yet too little is known about all the forms of financing. Venture capital garners the most attention and share of mind, and it is the primary form of financing after a very early point in a company's lifecycle. But venture capital isn't the only choice, and it may not be the optimal one, especially at each step it's available. My goal in writing this book is to help founders understand the various options for financing, and how each could impact their business.

To people outside the somewhat cloistered world of Silicon Valley, the multimillion- (sometimes billion-) dollar figures that get thrown around are unimaginable. (I'm using "Silicon Valley" not just literally, but also figuratively, as it's as much a specific place as a stand-in for anywhere that has a vibrant innovation ecosystem – New York, Seattle, Boston, Austin, etc.) But these valuations aren't arbitrary. They're based on sophisticated methodologies that take into account intellectual property, current revenue, projections about growth and scalability, future profitability, and risk.

Risk is how venture capitalists justify getting so much equity, the amount of risk they take on being proportional to the potential reward. That's a fair point. But making sure investors who take risk early on get handsomely rewarded and allowing entrepreneurs to keep more control of their companies is not an either/or proposition.

This isn't a criticism of venture capitalists or the fundamentals of the venture-capital model. Many of the companies that have changed the way we live, work, communicate, and function in every aspect of our lives – individually and collectively, in business-to-business (B2B) and business-to-consumer (B2C) – would not have succeeded without venture capital. That's especially true of companies that have been formed within the past 30 years.

Venture capitalists are essential to the success of the U.S. innovation ecosystem, not only because of the money they provide, but also for the business acumen, connections, and cachet they bring to fledgling companies.

For many years, I was a venture capitalist, so I say this with conviction. *Forbes* put me on their "Midas List" of the most successful VCs several years running. My former colleagues and I did work I am proud of. I loved sitting on the boards of startup companies and helping entrepreneurs succeed; there was a rush knowing that the businesses we were financing could make a real difference.

But along the way I started to see that there was another way to help startups get much-needed capital, and that's through debt. Debt can take several different forms: it can be a loan against accounts receivable and/or inventory (an asset-based loan – ABL); an advance on predictable revenue (such as monthly recurring revenue – MRR); a percentage of future, less-predictable revenue (a revenue-based loan – RBL); or in the form of venture debt – loans to venture-backed companies that have yet to reach profitability. This can happen at almost any stage at which a company would consider taking venture capital. My company, Runway Growth Capital, makes loans to later-stage, pre-profit companies.

Using debt as an alternative to or in conjunction with raising additional venture capital is an unfamiliar concept to many people and consequently isn't used often enough. (To be clear, "venture capital" and "venture capitalists," i.e., "VCs," refer to providing equity to startups in exchange for an ownership stake in the company; "venture debt" and "venture lenders" refer to providing loans, which results in less dilution.)

Debt, like just about any other financial instrument, can be a lever, used to propel something forward, or it can be a hammer, brought down with enough force to be destructive. Taking debt at the appropriate time, under the right terms, from someone you've vetted as carefully as they've vetted you, can open a world of possibilities for you and your business.

While finalizing the manuscript for this book, something unthinkable happened. Silicon Valley Bank failed and was taken over by the FDIC following a run on the bank. Thousands of startups and VCs had rushed to withdraw their cash out of SVB amid worries that the bank's assets (severely impaired as a result of rapidly rising interest rates) would not be sufficient to cover its liabilities.

This will undoubtedly change the landscape and impact the way that startups are funded and manage their financial affairs. There will be more on this later in the book, and you will be able to find ongoing updates on the book's website.

I understand the pressures entrepreneurs face: worrying about meeting payroll, wondering if others will buy into your vision, and navigating the internal struggle between being convinced you have a great idea and being frustrated with the time it can take to nurture a growing company to success. While I have never run a technology startup, I have started several businesses as well as a number of investment funds.

I've had to face wrenching decisions about which team members to let go; how much risk I and the remaining team could and should continue to absorb; and there have been times that I've wondered whether it was all worth it. I've lost enough money to keep me awake at night and paid heavy prices personally: losing time with my children; enduring stress on my relationships; and seeing friendships suffer, either because I was too busy or because of the complications that arise when you inevitably become friends with people with whom you work.

My own experiences have given me valuable insights into the issues founders face, personally and professionally, and that's why I'm confident that this book will be helpful to you, regardless of what stage you and your business are at. If you've got an idea locked somewhere in your brain that you haven't brought to the surface yet, this will help you navigate the entire financial journey. If you're in the formative stage, still looking for your first funding, this book will be useful, because it's never too soon to start thinking about how to fund the scaleup that comes after the startup.

And if you've been around for a while, with a promising but still not profitable business, it's definitely time for you to think about alternatives for financing. Doing the same kind of deal again and again – taking dilutive rounds of venture capital – might not be the best solution for you and your business.

In *All Money Is Not Created Equal*, I'll give you an overview of the startup world: a look at the ecosystem, how money moves through it, how to evaluate capitalization options, and how to assess a funding partner, and I will help you understand the implications of different types of money.

Throughout the book, I'll be sharing my own experiences, such as bringing part of Runway Growth Capital public, as well as including stories about companies and deals that will bring various points to life. You'll also find a glossary of words and phrases commonly used in the world of startups and VCs.

You won't find advice on how to be a great leader or the latest thinking in management. There are scores of excellent books already written on how to manage your team. But I will tell you what to be aware of as you build your team and offer advice on how to manage yourself – what you need to think about, consider, and be aware of along the way – in the context of how these things can affect funding, financial stability, and your startup's potential for growth. You'll find useful information rather than advice; my goal is to teach, not preach.

The book is organized into sections with easily digestible chapters, and key points are summarized at the end of each chapter. While I hope that you will read the entire chapter – and the whole book – these summaries can help you decide which chapters will be of the most immediate interest and use to you. You'll find some repetition of explanations throughout the book, which was intentional, knowing that the book may be consumed in phases.

You'll notice that, once I've introduced someone, instead of subsequently referring to them by their last name, I've opted for the rather unorthodox practice of referring to them by their first names. These people are partners, friends, colleagues; it seems impersonal to me to refer to them otherwise.

This book will help you understand that "all money is not created equal" and what the implications of that idea are for you and your business.

# Part One

## Setting the Stage

# Chapter 1

## A Tale of Two Companies

To help you better understand the difference between venture capital and venture debt, I'm going to start with a fictitious case study about the choices two growing companies made for getting capital. Throughout this book, as much as possible, I'll be using lessons drawn from actual companies and my own experiences (even though I may be masking the actual identities of the companies/individuals involved).

For the sake of simplicity, I am inventing two fictional examples. We'll call them 4Paws and 19/39. (You'll be seeing more about these two made-up companies throughout the book. In some instances, it will not be appropriate to use actual financial details from real companies; in other cases, examples from real companies would make those companies too easily identified.)

Recently, biotech has been one of the hottest areas in VC, but it wasn't as hot in the first decade of the twenty-first century, when our two imaginary companies were founded. However, there were some big, real-life winners in those years: 23andMe, the popular genetics company, was started in 2006; Acceleron Pharma was founded in 2003, went public 10 years later, and was acquired by Merck & Co. in 2021 for $11.5 billion; and StemCentrx was founded in 2008, and less than 10 years later was sold to AbbVie for $5.8 billion.[1]

---

[1] https://www.crunchbase.com/organization/stem-centrx (accessed September 11, 2022).

Our fictitious companies, 4Paws Corporation and 19/39, Inc., were veterinary biotechs (19/39 took its name from the fact that cats have 19 sets of chromosomes and dogs have 39). The companies had similar goals: to maximize the amount of information that could be learned about cats and dogs from their genetic material and determine which information would be most valuable, and to whom.

Joshua Nickerson, founder of 4Paws, and Jens Ley, founder of 19/39, had a friendly rivalry. They had worked together in senior positions at Damascene Sciences, an early (also-fictional) biotech success in Silicon Valley, where they both had been early employees. Both Nickerson and Ley initiated operations in 2006 using their own savings, including money made from option grants of Damascene stock, as seed money. (Their own significant investments allowed them to avoid going the typical "friends and family" route and/or raising initial capital from seed/angel investors, luxuries real-life founders seldom have.)

After brief ramp-up periods where the founders continued to self-fund their companies, both companies completed their Series-A rounds in 2007, with each raising $5 million at $10 million pre-money valuation, for post-funding valuation figures of $15 million each. (In venture-speak, "pre-money valuation" + "new money" = "post-money valuation.")

So, in the cases of 4Paws and 19/39, the VC investors paid $5 million to own 33.33% of each company ($5 million of new money being 33.33% of the post-money valuation of $15 million). Nickerson and Ley each owned 33.33% of their respective companies, with the remaining one-third of each company allocated or reserved for current and future employees (either directly or through the employee stock-option pool). (See the following simple capitalization table, commonly referred to as a "cap table"):

|  | Series A |
| --- | --- |
| Source of Capital | VCs |
| | |
| **Amount of Capital and Valuation** | |
| Pre-$ | $10,000 |
| New-$ | $5,000 |
| Post-$ | $15,000 |
| | |
| **What You Give Up** | |
| Dilution | 33% |
| | |
| **Who Owns What** | |
| Series C Preferred Stock | |
| Series B Preferred Stock | |
| Series A Preferred Stock | 33% |
| Founders* | 33% |
| Employees* | 33% |
| | 100% |

*Common stock and option pool

Note: Numbers don't necessarily add up to 100 because of rounding.

By 2012, after five years and two more rounds of venture funding (Series B and Series C), each company had shown promising results with the analysis that could be done with just one vial of blood from either a cat or a dog. Information about likely disease markers and preventive medicines and changes in diet proved to be valuable to veterinarians, pet insurers, and pet owners.

Some readers will (rightly) point out that they have seen valuations between rounds increase much faster than in our examples. We are being conservative and attempting to model "normal" times. Obviously the higher the valuation, the less dilution to founders, management, and early investors. However, the dangers of raising equity capital at inflated, unsupportable, and unrealistic valuations are well known and far outweigh the short-term gratification of a "silly" valuation.

|  | Series A | Series B | Series C |
|---|---|---|---|
| Source of Capital | VCs | VCs | VCs |
| **Amount of Capital and Valuation** |  |  |  |
| Pre-$ | $10,000 | $20,000 | $40,000 |
| New-$ | $5,000 | $10,000 | $20,000 |
| Post-$ | $15,000 | $30,000 | $60,000 |
| **What You Give Up** |  |  |  |
| Dilution | 33% | 33% | 33% |
| **Who Owns What** |  |  |  |
| Series C Preferred Stock |  |  | 33% |
| Series B Preferred Stock |  | 33% | 22% |
| Series A Preferred Stock | 33% | 22% | 15% |
| Founders* | 33% | 22% | 15% |
| Employees* | 33% | 22% | 15% |
|  | 100% | 100% | 100% |

*Common stock and option pool

Note: Numbers don't necessarily add up to 100 because of rounding.

Considering that spending on cats and dogs was estimated to be at least $50 billion per year at the time (and by 2018 was expected to grow to approximately $72 billion), both companies were attracting attention from investment bankers and potential acquirers, ranging from pet insurers to veterinary pharma companies to pet-food companies.

In 2013, neither company was yet profitable, and each raised its Series D round of financing and further refined its scope of research. 4Paws was looking for ways to monetize the data it had already collected to generate more revenue. Nickerson hoped that eventually 4Paws could collect enough data to be able to figure out what diet changes could help both prevent and treat diseases in animals and prolong their lives, using "food as medicine."

| | Series A | Series B | Series C | Series D |
|---|---|---|---|---|
| Source of Capital | VCs | VCs | VCs | Growth Investors |
| Amount of Capital and Valuation | | | | |
| Pre-$ | $10,000 | $20,000 | $40,000 | $75,000 |
| New-$ | $5,000 | $10,000 | $20,000 | $30,000 |
| Post-$ | $15,000 | $30,000 | $60,000 | $105,000 |
| What You Give Up | | | | |
| Dilution | 33% | 33% | 33% | 29% |
| Who Owns What | | | | |
| Series D Preferred Stock | | | | 29% |
| Series C Preferred Stock | | | 33% | 24% |
| Series B Preferred Stock | | 33% | 22% | 16% |
| Series A Preferred Stock | 33% | 22% | 15% | 11% |
| Founders* | 33% | 22% | 15% | 11% |
| Employees* | 33% | 22% | 15% | 11% |
| | 100% | 100% | 100% | 100% |

*Common stock and option pool

Note: Numbers don't necessarily add up to 100 because of rounding.

Two years later, in 2015, 4Paws had reached a crossroads. Nickerson could see that profitability was years away, and the company had made little progress on proving the validity of the idea of "food as medicine." The tests and the resulting reports were expensive for consumers, and pet insurers had yet to be convinced to pick up the costs of either the tests or the reports. (One of the venture investors had hoped that lobbying efforts with the insurance companies would result in this change in coverage, but pet insurers remained leery.)

Weighing the options – including taking additional VC money – and recognizing the costs and risks of continuing along a path of unknown duration, Nickerson and his seven-member board (consisting of four VCs, two independent directors, and Nickerson, who was the chairman and CEO), decided to sell 4Paws. The VCs were no longer convinced that 4Paws had blockbuster potential, meaning raising additional capital would have been difficult. 4Paws was sold for $100 million to the (fictional) Unicorn Pet Food Company. The aspirationally and prophetically named Unicorn had been founded in 1997. After going public in 2007, it had grown consistently through shrewd acquisitions.

Nickerson, who still owned an 11% stake in 4Paws after four rounds of venture capital, received consideration of $10 million in cash. Fortunately, Nickerson had negotiated with his VC investors to have their investment be in the form of nonparticipating preferred stock versus participating preferred stock, which gives the VCs their money back and then their share (based on ownership percentage) of proceeds above their investment. This method almost treats the preferred stock as debt in the sense that it must be repaid before profits are allocated among the owners. You can see why it's called double dipping.

| (in millions) | | |
|---|---|---|
| Purchase price | $100,000 | |
| Fees and expenses | $2,500 | |
| Proceeds to shareholders | $97,500 | |
| | Participating Preferred Stock | Non-participating Preferred Stock |
| Proceeds | $97,500 | $97,500 |
| VC Liquidation Preference | $65,000 | 0 |
| | $32,500 | $97,500 |

| Allocation of Net Proceeds | | | |
| --- | --- | --- | --- |
| Series D Preferred Stock | 29% | $9,286 | $27,857 |
| Series C Preferred Stock | 24% | $7,738 | $23,214 |
| Series B Preferred Stock | 16% | $5,159 | $15,476 |
| Series A Preferred Stock | 11% | $3,439 | $10,317 |
| Founders | 11% | $3,439 | $10,316 |
| Employees | 11% | $3,439 | $10,318 |
| | 100% | | |

During this same time frame, 19/39 had gone in a different direction. In 2012, 19/39 had started selling cat food, "Felin' Fine," through veterinary practices and at high-end animal boutiques. Although the food was not yet clinically proven to neutralize dander and reduce allergic reactions in humans, studies with both humans and cats looked promising. And anecdotal information among the cat-owning community suggested the food did indeed have a dander-dampening effect.

While 19/39 made no such claims about the food, it certainly benefited from the endorsement by the vocal online cat-owning community, which swore to Felin' Fine's allergen-reducing powers. The company decided to narrow its focus to cats, as that line of research was proving more promising than research connected to dogs. Also, sales of Felin' Fine were surging because of its presumed and proclaimed – but not yet proven – benefits regarding allergies.

Ley's company also became an acquisition target for Unicorn Pet Food. Like 4Paws, 19/39 was not yet profitable; at the time of the offer from Unicorn in 2015, 19/39 was valued at approximately $85 million. Ley was confident that proving the science behind neutralizing cat dander was close and that selling for $85 million would mean leaving many, many millions on the table. Plus, $85 million was lower than the valuation of his most recent round of venture capital, and he didn't want to disappoint his investors.

The quest for the dander-neutralizing agent had been and would continue to be expensive, but Ley and his board also knew that, if found, it would be a game-changer. In 2015, there were an estimated 86.4 million cats living in U.S. households, and given the prevalence of cat allergies, the market potential for Felin' Fine was enormous. There was also the idea that 19/39 could sell adjacent products for feline fans: other kinds of cat food; cat litter; and cat accessories, including furniture such as climbing posts and beds.

The challenge was making sure that the ingredient that neutralized Fel d 1, the protein that is the primary source of allergens, would be seen as a food additive and not as a medicine. If it remained as a food additive, it would be widely available to cat owners without the expense of going to a veterinarian and getting a prescription, and the food itself would be available without a prescription.

As the company considered Unicorn's buyout offer as well as the risks and rewards of remaining independent, one of 19/39's VC board members, Laura Taitt, suggested that Ley explore venture debt to fund the company and allow it to remain independent as opposed to taking on another round of venture capital. Additional VC money would further dilute Ley's stake in the company as well as the stakes of early VC investors (including Taitt, an investor in the Series A round). Also, another round of venture capital would mean bringing on at least one more board member.

After 10 years of investing in the company, the early investors had no more capital available ("dry powder" in VC slang) to support the company. Taitt and Ley both believed that the value of 19/39 could increase dramatically, but the company needed more time – more runway – before its cash ran out.

Raising growth capital without the additional ownership dilution and governance strings of more venture capital sounded great to Ley; however, he had never heard of venture debt. Taitt explained that venture debt was a type of loan that basically promised the assets of the company as collateral, much as a house would be the collateral for a mortgage.

Banks lend against the value of a home because of their belief in the borrower's ability to repay the loan, and because they will have a presumably valuable asset to seize if the debt isn't paid off. Venture lenders' thinking is somewhat similar: loans are made against the enterprise value of the business.

Companies use the proceeds for important strategic initiatives, such as shoring up its sales and marketing functions, perhaps making it a more attractive acquisition target; financing a critical aspect of the company's next stage of growth; or making its own strategic acquisition. The use will largely depend on at what stage of its growth the company borrows money.

Ultimately, in 2015, 19/39 borrowed $30 million from Pioneer Growth Credit Fund (a fictitious venture-debt lender). Ley had also investigated taking additional venture capital and had term sheets for equity, making it easy to compare the cost of venture equity versus venture debt. The interest rate on his loans from Pioneer was 10.2%: LIBOR (of 0.2%) + 1,000 bps.

Raising $30 million in a Series E round at its 2015 valuation of $85 million would have meant doing a down round (where the valuation is lower than the previous round, sending negative signals to investors, employees, and potentially customers and partners) and causing more than 25% dilution for Ley, his management team, employees, and existing shareholders. Using venture debt in 2015 provided 19/39 with the $30 million it needed but resulted in less than 1.5% dilution (the amount needed for warrant coverage).

Using equity in 2015 would have been highly dilutive and a down round.

|  | Series A | Series B | Series C | Series D | Series E |
|---|---|---|---|---|---|
| Source of Capital | VCs | VCs | VCs | Growth Investors | Growth Investors |
| **Amount of Capital and Valuation** |  |  |  |  |  |
| Pre-$ | $10,000 | $20,000 | $40,000 | $75,000 | $85,000 |
| New-$ | $5,000 | $10,000 | $20,000 | $30,000 | $30,000 |
| Post-$ | $15,000 | $30,000 | $60,000 | $105,000 | $115,000 |
| **What You Give Up** |  |  |  |  |  |
| Dilution | 33% | 33% | 33% | 29% | 26% |
| **Who Owns What** |  |  |  |  |  |
| Series E Preferred Stock |  |  |  |  | 26% |
| Series D Preferred Stock |  |  |  | 29% | 21% |
| Series C Preferred Stock |  |  | 33% | 24% | 18% |
| Series B Preferred Stock |  | 33% | 22% | 16% | 12% |
| Series A Preferred Stock | 33% | 22% | 15% | 11% | 8% |
| Founders* | 33% | 22% | 15% | 11% | 8% |
| Employees* | 33% | 22% | 15% | 11% | 8% |
|  | 100% | 100% | 100% | 100% | 100% |

*Common stock and option pool

Note: Numbers don't necessarily add up to 100 because of rounding.

Using venture debt in 2015 provided the needed capital with minimal dilution (approximately 1.4% versus >25% with equity). Venture lenders normally ask for a small sliver of equity in the form of warrants to provide upside on their investment (known as an equity "kicker"). The amount of warrants is calculated using the "coverage" percentage you negotiate with your lender. For a late-stage company such as 19/39 the coverage would normally be between 2% and 5%. For riskier deals, it could be higher.

In the case of 19/39 we have assumed a 5% coverage so the dilution would be calculated as follows: $30 million loan × 5% = $1.5 million (the amount of equity the lender has the right to buy). This right to buy equity will be documented as a warrant, normally with a 10-year life, allowing the lender to purchase $1.5 million of equity in the most recent round at the price per share of that round. Here, that's $1.5 million at $105 million valuation or 1.4% dilution.

Ley also considered another advantage of venture debt: not having to add another board member in exchange for VC money. The board, consisting of five members, was an affable group with good chemistry; why ruin a good thing?

Taitt made the case that investing in the research and studies to be able to claim Felin' Fine was effective would be the best use of the $30 million in fresh capital. The rest of the board agreed, and a small team of highly trained scientists was hired. Within three years, they shepherded Felin' Fine through the necessary studies and the food could be marketed for its proven allergen-reducing qualities.

By February 2018, the product was ready for the mass market, and an additional $15 million in venture debt was taken on to invest in marketing the food on a wide scale. Because 19/39's value had increased and the risk of the loan had decreased, Pioneer Growth Credit was happy to increase the size of its loan and reduce the interest rate spread from 1,000 bps to 800 bps. They asked for no additional warrants for this new loan.

And by taking on debt rather than using equity, additional dilution had largely been avoided. Within six months, more than 10 million units of Felin' Fine had been sold, and 19/39 again became an acquisition target.

|  | Series A | Series B | Series C | Series D | Debt |
|---|---|---|---|---|---|
| **Source of Capital** | VCs | VCs | VCs | Growth Investors | Growth Lender |
| **Amount of Capital and Valuation** | | | | | |
| Pre-$ | $10,000 | $20,000 | $40,000 | $75,000 | $105,000 |
| New-$ | $5,000 | $10,000 | $20,000 | $30,000 | $30,000 |
| Post-$ | $15,000 | $30,000 | $60,000 | $105,000 | $105,000 |
| **What You Give Up** | | | | | |
| Dilution | 33% | 33% | 33% | 29% | 1.4% |
| **Who Owns What** | | | | | |
| Venture Debt Warrants | | | | | 1% |
| Series D Preferred Stock | | | | 29% | 28% |
| Series C Preferred Stock | | | 33% | 24% | 23% |
| Series B Preferred Stock | | 33% | 22% | 16% | 16% |
| Series A Preferred Stock | 33% | 22% | 15% | 11% | 10% |
| Founders* | 33% | 22% | 15% | 11% | 10% |
| Employees* | 33% | 22% | 15% | 11% | 10% |
|  | 100% | 100% | 100% | 100% | 100% |

*Common stock and option pool

Note: Numbers don't necessarily add up to 100 because of rounding.

In early 2019, 19/39 was sold for $400 million in a stock and cash deal to HealthEpets, a pet food company that also owned one of the largest pet insurers in the United States. Ley's 10% stake was worth approximately $40 million – a far cry from the $8 million Ley would have received if he had sold the company in 2015, when it was valued at $85 million.

By twice using venture debt instead of equity, Ley ultimately avoided approximately 25% dilution to the ownership positions of himself, his management, employees, and existing investors. This group kept $90 million that otherwise would have gone to a late-stage, quick-flip equity investor.

Now, I realize no one is going to cry for Nickerson, who walked away with $10 million when he sold 4Paws. But less important than the money to Nickerson was the fact that Unicorn didn't pursue the idea of "food as medicine" for animals. Instead, despite Nickerson's pleas, Unicorn abandoned his vision and used the 4Paws data to improve its marketing to pet owners.

Nickerson waited out his two-year noncompete and during that time he focused on his animal-rights activism. In 2020, he started a company that was looking at vitamin/CBD/kratom supplements for animals.

So, in 2020, you had very different outcomes for the founders and their two companies that had started out on similar paths. Nickerson had sold his company earlier, had no voice in his former company's future, and had gotten $10 million. Ley, on the other hand, received $40 million in 2019 and he and his company made a significant contribution to the well-being of millions of animals and their owners.

Had Ley sold in 2015 (as Nickerson did), the pursuit of his vision would have been out of his hands. As Nickerson found out, the promises of corporate acquirers are often quickly forgotten, leaving founders helpless spectators as others decide what will become of their passions. By using venture debt and staying independent, Ley succeeded in both realizing his dream and hitting a home run financially.

I've simplified the fictitious story here to help you understand the impact of financing decisions, that there are numerous formulas for capitalizing a company, and that there is no one-size-fits-all approach.

Throughout this book I'm going to try to help you understand more about venture capital and venture debt and the impact each can have on the viability and survival of your company as well as your ability to meet your goals. Too few people – whether they are founders, board members, or investors – think enough or even know enough about all the options. Debt – at the right time, in the right amount, from the right partner, under the right circumstances – can be a terrific option.

"Option" – as in choice – is the key word here. Debt is not always the solution, and not every company that takes on debt will have the same kind of satisfying result imagined for 19/39. But such outcomes are possible; I've seen them happen and helped make them happen.

It's also important to realize that using debt wasn't the only difference in the outcomes for Nickerson and Ley. There were other strategic decisions, such as 19/39's pivots to creating and selling cat food and to focusing exclusively on cats, that also affected their respective outcomes. In the appropriate chapters, I'll go into more detail about how decisions and actions each founder and company made at critical junctures affected their fortunes.

In the next chapter, I'll talk more about my journey from being a venture capitalist to becoming a growth lender supplying venture debt, helping companies grow and entrepreneurs achieve their ambitions.

## Key Takeaways

- Taking multiple rounds of venture capital will reduce a founder's stake in their company.
- A reduced stake will not only mean less money when an exit event occurs, but less (or no) control over execution of the founder's vision.
- Venture debt is an alternative to venture capital that will extend the runway for a not-yet-profitable company and reduce further dilution of ownership.

# Chapter 2

## All About Growth: My Journey from Venture Capital to Venture Debt

For most of my adult life I have been obsessed with providing companies with the capital they need to grow. For much of that time, I did it in very traditional ways: first as an investment banker, then as a venture capitalist. In 2010, after more than 20 years of investing in companies in exchange for equity, I came to see the light about the vital – and underappreciated – role of debt in funding growth at pre-profit companies.

While I've always been focused on helping companies grow, my route to venture debt was unintentional – and somewhat tumultuous – but has proven highly rewarding.

In 1989, I left investment banking to join the asset-management subsidiary of the British bank Lloyds Bank plc, where I was responsible for strategy and venture capital (VC) investing. In October 1989 and January 1990, I made my first two venture investments. The first one failed; the second one worked out spectacularly well – a 1,470.4% internal rate of return (IRR) and 464.8× multiple on invested capital (MOIC) in a span of 26 months.

When I moved from investment banking to the money-management world to focus on venture-capital investing, the executive who ran the investment-banking business tried to convince me not to go. "All you're going to be doing is dealing with problems," he warned me.

That isn't how I saw it. To me, investment banking was a transactional business, and venture capital represented a chance to build a business focused on relationships rather than transactions.

Bankers do "deals" (raise capital, buy or sell something, etc.), which requires active engagement for a short period of time, typically several months. VCs, on the other hand, will often be intimately involved with a portfolio company for anywhere from three to 20 years.

For venture investors who lead rounds and take board seats (like I did), the relationship is particularly close and intensely satisfying. (You'll read more about this in Chapters 8 and 17.) Startups have problems, but helping entrepreneurs solve problems sounded exciting.

After three years of intense strategy and corporate development work, the portion of my time focused on venture investing gradually increased to the point where I was working full-time as a VC. Using a portion of the assets of our parent company's family of mutual funds, throughout 1993, 1994, and 1995, I invested in more than a dozen additional companies. The performance of those investments was very strong. I focused on building a diversified portfolio targeting three sectors—technology, communications, and healthcare—for a three-legged-stool strategy.

Along the way, I learned about syndicates, down rounds, recaps, pay-to-play, and other nuances of the opaque world of venture capital. (All of these terms, and others, are explained in the Glossary section of the Appendix.)

By 1995, based on my success using mutual-fund capital, I was able to launch a standalone venture capital fund (Fund I) aimed at attracting outside investors. This fund was structured as a limited partnership. Some of our first investors were Bernard Arnault, CEO of French luxury goods company LVMH, and the Massachusetts Bay Transit Authority. In February 1995, I made the first investment for Fund I in a telecommunications infrastructure company called Ciena Corporation (for its Series-B round). We also invested in Ciena's Series C in December 1995 and sold our shares following the company's IPO in February 1997, earning an IRR of 643.4% and a MOIC of 105.3×. We raised Fund II in 1997.

The results of our investments from 1995 to 2000 were incredible. In 1998, after prolonged, acrimonious negotiations between me and the man who had been my mentor, my team and I bought the business from Lloyds Bank plc and renamed the ensuing company Crescendo Ventures. Crescendo raised Funds III and IV, in

1998 and 2000, with $250 million and $650 million, respectively. During that period, my family and Crescendo moved from Minneapolis to the Bay Area.

If I wanted to be a player, I needed to be where the game was being played. The heart and soul of venture capital, innovation, and entrepreneurship were – and still are – in Silicon Valley. So I moved my family to California – getting half the house for twice the price – set up shop in Palo Alto, and attempted to make a name for myself in Silicon Valley and on Sand Hill Road. (Sand Hill Road is the actual street where many of the VCs are located, but it's also a catch-all address, just as Wall Street is in financial services; K Street is in lobbying; and Madison Avenue is in advertising.)

The adjustments of the move to Silicon Valley took their toll on me and my family. The "breakup" with my mentor was very painful. He had given me the opportunity to branch out and try different things, and his confidence in me was the fuel that moved me forward. I had thought it was a relationship built on mutual respect and trust, but when I realized it was time to move on, his initial show of support proved false. He made things immeasurably more difficult by saying things like "My word is my bond, but it's not binding." (To this day, I still can't understand that sentence.)

The move from Minneapolis was difficult for a variety of reasons. My wife (now my ex-wife) and I had two children under the age of two, and we were leaving behind family (including our children's grandparents), friends, and all that was familiar. Silicon Valley is a competitive, demanding place. I got caught up in the frenetic pace and it seemed like the business absorbed all my time and attention. My then-wife was left largely on her own to raise our kids, without the benefit and comfort of having extended family nearby. I'm not proud when I say I too often chose business over family and missed out on countless memories that can never be recaptured.

That said, would I do it differently knowing what I know now? Honestly, it's hard to say. I'm grateful that I have good relationships today with my children, I'm happily remarried, and I'm at a point in my career where I've been able to see the returns on my investment – both financial and otherwise – and enjoy them.

But I don't know if I would have been able to achieve what I set out to do without working as hard as I did or being so singularly focused. This is not a journey for the faint of heart.

Part of what was driving not only me but the frenetic pace of Silicon Valley in the late 1990s was the staggering velocity of money. Of course, this was also the first wave of e-commerce and other internet-related businesses. Companies were going public in less than three years from their first venture-capital investments. At the time, investors believed that internet traffic was doubling every 100 days and that the world's communications networks needed to be upgraded to handle the load.

Investors were betting hundreds of billions of dollars that the existing communications networks, largely based on copper wires, would need to be replaced by high-speed fiber-optic cables and wireless communication technologies. Communications investing was hot and Crescendo Ventures was one of the world's leading VC firms focused on communications technology. By 1999, we had dropped our "third leg of the stool" – healthcare investing – to focus exclusively on tech and telecom.

Until late 2000, our portfolio companies were routinely being valued at 100× revenues; we were investors in three of the largest and hottest IPOs of 2000 (Cosine, Corvis, and Oplink). On paper, the value of our funds (and my share of the profits) was enormous.

Unfortunately, the party didn't last long. When Nortel (one of the largest publicly traded communications technology companies) missed its third-quarter earnings in 2000, the comm tech bubble burst – and so did ours. The meltdown was dramatic and painful, with the NASDAQ Telecom index dropping 95%. Reflecting on the state of the industry over Thanksgiving 2000, I knew we needed to prepare for a rough ride.

Even as the meltdown was occurring and I was losing an enormous amount of money, at least on paper, I could occasionally stand back and appreciate the amazing and thrilling journey I had experienced building a venture business over the previous 10 years. I could also see that the future would be different. But nothing I had learned over that decade could prepare me for how traumatic and difficult the next five years would be.

Crescendo responded aggressively to the market problems. We developed groundbreaking models for risk-profile management and scenario analysis; culled the portfolio; doubled down on the best companies; downsized the team; and eventually pivoted to a new strategy, focusing on more capital-efficient, highly disruptive technology companies. All of this was painful. We had experienced enormous success, and it was hard to reconcile the losses we had experienced with the picture we had of ourselves as visionaries. Had our success been merely a case of the rising tide lifting all boats? Were we any smarter – or less smart – than anyone else out there?

As good as you feel when you've been successful, you feel twice as bad when things go south. You doubt yourself and everything you've ever believed or taken for granted about who you are. You have to lay off people you swore you'd go to hell and back with. You not only have to rethink the future, but you do so with the added burden of questioning the past.

Amid the tumult, I was able to maintain a certain level of dispassionate focus. One of the things that really stood out to me amid this bloodbath was the fact that while the equity investors in our technology companies were losing their shirts, the lenders – those who were involved on the debt side – were often getting paid back.

Throughout the aughts, my partners and I worked to salvage and build value in Crescendo IV. We were fortunate that our limited partners believed in us enough to allow us to recycle funds to continue to invest to build value. Recycling occurs when the investors in venture funds allow the VC to retain and reinvest proceeds on exits (sale of portfolio companies) rather than distribute the proceeds to the limited partners.

As we were working to earn our way out of the hole created by the implosion of the communications industry and rebuild value in Crescendo IV, I made several new investments, which (thankfully) produced excellent results. After more than a decade of work recovering value, the fund is likely rated in the top quartile for an early 2000-vintage communications-focused fund.

However, raising a new venture-capital fund wasn't an option. As much as our investors were appreciative of our work to maximize the value of Crescendo IV, they weren't willing to provide capital to form Crescendo V. It was humbling to face the fact that people wouldn't give us more money. It also made us realize that we needed a new approach to funding entrepreneurs.

They say that necessity is the mother of invention. For us, staying in the game of funding entrepreneurs building important companies necessitated finding a new way to do it. We felt that there had to be a structure that would meet the needs of these founders while delivering an attractive return profile to us and our investors. We concluded that the next big innovation in funding growth companies could be, and should be, the use of debt as an alternative to equity. We saw debt as our path forward, despite the negative connotations that debt often has.

Our realization that debt was the logical alternative was based on years of listening to entrepreneurs' pitches and seeing hundreds of companies seeking financing but not fitting the venture-capital profile for one of two reasons:

1. They couldn't attract investment because the potential for growth of the business wasn't exciting enough for VCs; or
2. They could get venture capital but didn't want it because they wouldn't accept VCs' terms. They didn't want to deal with the governance terms (board seats, revesting shares, the potential to be fired from their own company) and/or the economic terms, which would mean dilution of their ownership stake.

Debt as an alternative to equity was attractive to us. We were willing to accept lower returns compared to what we might get with equity if providing the debt came both with lower risk and more predictable, nearer-term cash flows than we would get with equity.

From the entrepreneurs' perspective, capital-raise alternatives need to be evaluated relative to the cost of giving up equity from both the economic and governance perspectives. On both fronts, debt is cheaper than equity.

I confess to wanting to be a resource for companies that were being passed over by VCs. As a firm of outsiders coming from Minneapolis and starting up in Silicon Valley, we were definitely underdogs against all the big guys. We felt a kind of affinity to the entrepreneur who was the underdog. We like helping underappreciated entrepreneurs see their dreams come to fruition.

The company that really opened my eyes to the possibilities of capitalization beyond venture capital was a business called Only Natural Pet (ONP) – a real company, not one of our fictional pet-tech businesses. In 2010, as we were reckoning with "What next?," ONP was the largest producer of organic pet food in the country.

ONP had never taken external venture-capital financing but did have both Small Business Administration (SBA) and local banking credit relationships (both of which had personal guarantees). ONP had a six-year history of profitable growth and was generating $10 million in revenue. The CEO, Martin Grosjean, Jr., wanted to grow even faster, but ONP needed additional capital to achieve more aggressive revenue growth.

ONP came to us because it had an opportunity to sign a nationwide deal with the retailer PetSmart. ONP went to its lenders and essentially said, "Hey, this is the chance of a lifetime. We can double our business because PetSmart wants to roll it out in a bunch of their stores at the same time. All we need to do is make the product to increase our inventory."

The company's existing lenders, including its bank, which had been with the company for some 10 years, declined to support the inventory build necessary to fulfill the opportunity with PetSmart. The bank didn't want to take on additional risk. ONP's CEO didn't want to raise equity because he knew the value of his business was about to balloon and taking equity would dilute his stake. ONP came to us looking for a solution to fund its additional expansion.

The timing was good, as we had been working with my brother, Kevin Spreng, a corporate/VC attorney, to develop a structure that minimized dilution and governance strings for the entrepreneur while simultaneously providing us (the investor) with a fair return. The structure we pioneered with Kevin (first used with ONP) later came to be known as a revenue-based loan (RBL). We thought ONP was an ideal fit for our new funding solution. To pursue this new RBL opportunity we formed a new firm, which we named Decathlon Capital Partners.

Using our capital, the company was able to fulfill a game-changing order with a national retailer. ONP wasn't a VC deal and it was already profitable, but it was still a great opportunity to support a deserving entrepreneur building an interesting business while generating a nice return for ourselves.

With the closing of the ONP deal in early 2011, our new firm, Decathlon Capital Partners, became a revenue-based lender, and my partners and I officially stopped being equity VCs and began our journey as growth lenders. Today, Decathlon is the largest RBL provider in the world.

The RBL approach to helping companies grow captured attention outside of Silicon Valley. In 2013, I was invited to be a speaker at the World Economic Forum annual meeting in Davos, Switzerland, as an "impact investor." We didn't set out to be impact investors. Decathlon is first and foremost a financial investor (i.e., it invests to generate financial returns commensurate with the risk it is taking). It's just that the paucity of providers of growth funding for small businesses (particularly for female and minority entrepreneurs) has resulted in anyone helping to fill this funding gap being labeled as an "impact investor."

Based on my presentation in Davos, I was invited by the Obama White House to speak to the Small Business Administration about what we were doing. I felt great not being just one of 500 VCs on Sand Hill Road but doing something innovative and different. It was very satisfying to see that our approach was making sense to the world at large.

There were all kinds of other financial innovations going on in Silicon Valley during this time as well. In 2010, the same year we developed the RBL structure, my good friend Michael Moe founded GSV Capital and asked me to join his board of directors. Michael formed GSV (which stands for Global Silicon Valley) to provide individual investors – as opposed to institutions – with a way to invest in companies before they went public.

Michael, the former head of growth equity research at Merrill Lynch, was one of the first people to understand that companies would opt to stay private longer. He predicted that where companies had often looked to go public when their valuation was a couple of hundred million dollars, going forward, companies would wait until their valuations were in the billions.

That meant that if individual investors wanted to participate in the increase in valuation from $200 million to somewhere in the billions (the new norm for IPOs), they needed a vehicle that would allow them to do so. Big institutional investors could invest privately, but for the most part, individual investors had no way to get in before the IPO. GSV was like a mutual fund whose portfolio was private, venture-backed companies.

Michael founded GSV Capital to buy shares of yet-to-be-public unicorns – private companies, almost always venture-backed – that are valued at a billion dollars or more. He acquired shares directly from founders or early investors and occasionally directly from the company and allowed individual investors to participate by investing in his fund, which was traded on NASDAQ. While sitting on his board I watched GSV invest pre-IPO in Facebook, Twitter, Palantir, Snap, Groupon, Spotify, Lyft, Chegg, Dropbox, and many other companies.

It struck me that these companies and thousands of others – including those not likely to become unicorns but with more than promising growth potential – would benefit from using debt, or more of it, to finance their growth. Even if companies weren't going to have valuations in the billions, why shouldn't they also have the opportunity to grow and increase their valuations with minimal dilution?

At the same time, my VC friends were telling me that they liked the idea of debt as an alternative to equity for late-stage companies – especially given that companies were staying private longer and needed more private capital. Unfortunately, Decathlon's RBL structure was not a good fit for late-stage venture-backed companies. VCs don't like the concept of a debt instrument that calls for payments that accelerate in line with a company's revenue growth. VCs look for and expect explosive growth in revenues, so linking the cost of capital to their most sacred metric, revenues, is antithetical to their business model.

As I was thinking about all these things, I started researching the venture debt industry. As a VC, I was aware of the key participants (Hercules, TriplePoint, WTI, and SVB), but I didn't value their role in the ecosystem. VCs (myself included at the time) view themselves as occupying a special position at the top of the food chain. I now know how misguided I was in ignoring the important role debt providers play in the Silicon Valley community.

At the time, like most VCs, I looked up to entrepreneurs, but looked down on almost everyone else. As I grew older and wiser and learned painful lessons the hard way, I began to see the value of debt providers. After more research, I began to understand the meaningful value proposition venture debt offers to growing companies *and* the attractive returns it provides to investors (because of the predictable cash flows and surprisingly low loss rates).

The more I pondered the emerging opportunity of venture debt, the more it intrigued me.

My friends encouraged me to combine my expertise from Crescendo (venture capital) and Decathlon (growth debt) to form a new fund to compete with Hercules Capital, Western Technology Investment (WTI), and TriplePoint Capital, the largest venture-debt firms in Silicon Valley.

My partners at Decathlon were perfectly happy doing their thing with RBLs, but I wanted to seize the opportunity to compete with the big guys while serving the kind of companies in which GSV was investing. So, in 2015 I founded GSV Growth Credit and amicably transitioned away from Decathlon.

After raising more capital than expected and attracting Oaktree Capital Management – the world's premier private credit firm, founded in 1995 by legendary investors Howard Marks and Bruce Karsh – as a key investor and strategic partner, in 2017 we changed the name of the firm from GSV to Runway Growth Capital.

Runway has grown quickly to become one of the largest, most active venture-debt players in the country, with offices in Silicon Valley, Chicago, New York, San Diego, Dallas, and Boston. We are honored to have partnered with many of the world's premier venture-capital firms in backing hundreds of passionate entrepreneurs in pursuit of their dreams and hope to continue to do so now that one of our funds is a publicly traded company. (Chapter 19 is a look at Runway's IPO journey.)

Over the years I have come to understand that venture debt isn't right for everybody. But for many companies (including those we serve at Runway), it is the most effective way to begin to introduce financial leverage to their businesses and use their balance sheets productively while avoiding unnecessary ownership dilution. Helping entrepreneurs discover and properly use venture debt has become my passion and the *raison d'être* of Runway Growth Capital.

## Key Takeaways

- There are numerous companies that deserve funding but have trouble attracting VCs' attention.
- More companies should consider venture debt as an alternative or complement to equity.
- Venture debt and revenue-based loans (RBLs) are two alternatives to venture capital that deserve more attention.

# Part Two

## Startups: Understanding the Arena

# Chapter 3

# The Stages of a Startup

*Thanks to having personal wealth from their stock options from Damascene, neither Nickerson of 4Paws nor Ley of 19/39 needed to go the "friends and family" or angel route for pre-seed or seed money. Each company transitioned from early stage (Series A and B) to late stage (Series C and beyond) after a five-year period. By their respective Series D fundings (seven years after initiating operations) each had achieved the critical milestone of being able to extract a considerable amount of information from just one vial of blood from both cats and dogs.*

*Two years after its Series D funding, Nickerson's 4Paws looked like it might be destined to linger in the late stage as it was clear that the company wasn't going to achieve blockbuster status, although it had several patents and some successes. It just wasn't going to be able to achieve its goal of making cat and dog food medicine. Nine years after starting his company, Nickerson sold, as his company wasn't able to attract the additional capital it needed to continue operating.*

*By contrast, Ley's 19/39 progressed to the growth stage. It wasn't yet profitable, but its product, Felin' Fine cat food, was popular and sales were ramping rapidly. As a result, VCs were eager to continue funding the company's ongoing investments in sales and marketing.*

*\*\*\**

Before we explore the stages of a startup, I want to establish how I am using that term. (I've borrowed from – and credited – other highly reliable sources for definitions that I think best describe many of the terms I use. When there is a good, strong, widely accepted definition it doesn't makes sense to reinvent the wheel.)

Investopedia's simple definition says, "The term startup refers to a company in the first stages of operations. Startups are founded by one or more entrepreneurs who want to develop a product or service for which they believe there is demand."[1] Nothing to argue with there, but that definition is a little too basic.

Many other definitions of a startup include highly aspirational elements, such as this one from *Forbes:* "Startups are businesses that want to disrupt industries and change the world – and do it all at scale. Startup founders dream of giving society something it needs but hasn't created yet – generating eye-popping valuations that lead to an initial public offering (IPO) and an astronomical return on investment."[2] We're getting closer.

According to *The Startup Owner's Manual,* "A startup is a temporary organization in search of a scalable, repeatable, profitable business model. Scalable startups are the work of traditional technology entrepreneurs. These entrepreneurs start a company believing their vision will change the world and result in a company with hundreds of millions, if not billions of dollars in sales."[3] That definition captures much of what distinguishes the kinds of companies I've been talking about from other nascent businesses.

Now that we know what a startup is, when is a company no longer a startup? My view is that a company stops being a startup when it achieves scale. How do we define scale? Alex Wilhelm of *TechCrunch* is credited with coining the "50-100-500 rule": you can no longer be defined as a startup if any one of these is true: you have revenue that exceeds $50 million, have 100 or more employees, or have a value of $500 million or more.

Given that Alex created this definition in 2014 when valuations were much lower, I think it could be adjusted to the "100-500-1,000 rule" where a company ceases to be a startup when it achieves $100 million in revenue, 500 employees, or $1 billion valuation. I realize there will be readers who argue that some of today's unicorns (valuation of $1 billion or greater) are

[1]https://www.investopedia.com/terms/s/startup.asp, accessed September 22, 2022.
[2]https://www.forbes.com/advisor/business/what-is-a-startup/ (accessed February 16, 2023).
[3]Bob Dorf and Steve Blank, *The Startup Owners' Manual* (K&S Ranch, 2012), xvii.

still startups. Perhaps. And, perhaps those companies should not be unicorns?

Most observers, myself included, break the lifecycle of startup into the following stages based on the level of funding achieved: seed, early, late, growth. I'm also going to talk about the "pre-seed" stage because even though you won't be taking VC money, you'll very likely be taking outside money, whether in the form of angel investments or investments, gifts, or loans from "friends and family." It would be highly unusual – and unlikely to be a smart decision – to take debt at the pre-seed or seed stage.

According to PitchBook and the National Venture Capital Association, who collaborate to produce the leading source of data on the venture capital industry, *PitchBook – NVCA Venture Monitor*, the four broad categories of growth are defined as follows:

1. **Seed-stage** rounds are defined as being less than $10 million and the first round of funding as reported by a government filing or when an investor or a press release refers to the funding as "seed." Although not tracked as such by PitchBook/NVCA, this stage can be further separated into pre-seed, seed, and seed-plus, as many startups raise three distinct funding rounds before their Series A. Seed-stage investors may be VCs, incubators, or angels.
2. **Early-stage** generally includes Series A or B funding.
3. **Late-stage** generally includes Series C or D or later funding.
4. **Growth-stage** rounds include at least one investor tagged as growth/expansion and are at least $15 million. Very often, these rounds are expected to be the last before an exit. Growth-stage investors are differentiated from private equity (PE) investors in that growth equity investments generally do not involve a change of control or large amounts of leverage financing (LBO debt), both of which are typical in PE deals.

Funding for companies in their earliest stages has changed considerably in the past decade or so. It used to be that the first round of financing for a company – beyond bootstrapping, self-funding, and friends and family – was the seed round. The money usually came from angels: wealthy individuals who invest their own money. There's now a pre-seed round, and you might see multiple seed rounds.

As Kyle Wong, co-founder of Pixlee TurnTo (now PixleeEmplifi) says, "The pre-seed or angel round is what the historical seed round was. And then the seed round today is what the A was, and it basically trickles down as a result."

Why did this shift happen? My view is that it's a direct result of VC firms raising larger and larger funds and finding that the economics and efficiency of doing small deals (as are typical in the seed stage) no longer made sense. Accordingly, a new feeder system was developed (angels, micro VCs, incubators, accelerators, etc.) to do the heavy lifting associated with the earliest stages of startup companies, thus allowing the (now larger) VC firms to invest at a point at which it was more effective (i.e., they could write a bigger check and use their time more efficiently).

In the pre-seed stage, your "company" could be as simple as a founder and an idea. I've seen the most embryonic of ideas based on knowledge of the market and the conviction that there is a big opportunity to attract money. Pre-seed plans run the gamut from notes scribbled on the back of a napkin to well-vetted pitch decks.

If you have market knowledge and the wherewithal to be able to surround yourself with top people, you'll have a level of credibility that can make a detailed business plan unnecessary. On the other hand, if you've come out of an incubator, you'll have written a plan and a presentation that you've practiced pitching repeatedly.

As Alec Wright, chief product officer at global innovation community One Valley, points out, investors are betting on the enthusiasm, personality, and charisma of the founder. "You're not looking for a minimally viable product in that pre-seed/angel phase," says Wright. "You're not even looking for much in the way of proof at that point, or revenue. If you've already got a track record – from having founded a company or being a superstar – your investors are also betting on that."

## What Funding Looks Like

# How to Raise Startup Capital*

### VENTURE CAPITAL

- ⊙ Institutional Capital — You have to grow your company with an exit plan for the business in mind (VCs have to return money to their investors too)
- ⊙ Expert Advice, Operational Support, Strong Network — VCs are different, each of them invest in specific sectors/geographies/stages
- ⊙ For tech companies that have a minimal viable product and early traction
- ⊙ Can be complemented or supplemented with a growth loan / venture debt to retain more equity and further extend runway to reach milestones

### ANGEL INVESTORS

- ⊙ Typically invest earlier than VCs — Individuals / Angel syndicates
- ⊙ Can be complemented or supplemented with a growth loan to retain more equity and further extend runway to reach milestones

### CROWDFUNDING

- ⊙ Open to the entire public to invest — Kickstarter, Indiegogo, Fundable, Republic, SeedInvest, StartEngine
- ⊙ Find supporters who are willing to pay early for your product — Create public interest (and demand) for your product
- ⊙ Good for marketing
- ⊙ Best for consumer businesses
- ⊙ Can be supplemented with a growth loan

## ACCELERATORS

- Pre-product
- Mentorship & operational support 24/7
- Fast-track to start a business
- Can be supplemented with a growth loan
- Great brand value for the next fundraising if an accelerator is reputable
  - Y Combinator, Techstars, StartX

## CONTESTS

- Free capital (if you win)
- Some non-financial conditions may apply
- Typically a small amount of money
- Usually good media coverage
- Can be supplemented with a growth loan

## GRANTS FROM GOVERNMENT

- The process is very bureaucratic and long
- Can apply to certain industries only (and typically requires specific qualifications)
- You do not have to pay back
  - Finance and support for your business on grants.gov
  - Small Business Innovation Research and Small Business Technology Transfer programs on sbir.gov
- Can be supplemented with a growth loan

## BOOTSTRAP

- Grow without raising outside equity, helping founders retain a larger stake
- Can be supplemented with a growth loan (terms and structure might vary drastically depending on the business)

* Note: depending on the circumstances of the company, debt can be used at any stage as a supplement, complement or replacement for equity.

At this stage, you wouldn't have raised money other than possibly from friends and family. What form that money takes is up to you and them. It could be a gift, a loan, or an investment.

You and the management team (which could be just you) will most likely set the business up in such a way that your new company will sell shares to investors in return for funding. Because startups are often eager to get going and haven't yet established a price for their shares, your first rounds of funding may be accomplished using a convertible note or a SAFE (simple agreement for future equity). Both structures are designed to allow you to bring in cash (and start spending it) before the final closing of the round. This way you can raise money before you even agree on a price for your shares (i.e., a valuation for the company). A convertible note specifies that the note will convert at a modest discount (10% to 25%) into the new round when it closes to incentivize investors to move quicker.

The SAFE structure was developed by Y Combinator to make funding seed-stage companies easier and less expensive. The SAFE was introduced in 2013 and is widely used by both YC and non-YC startups. (You can read about the various models of a SAFE at the Y Combinator site: https://www.ycombinator.com/documents#about.)

Thomson Reuters defines a SAFE as "an investment contract between a startup and an investor that gives the investor the right to receive equity of the company on certain triggering events, such as a:

- Future equity financing (known as a Next Equity Financing or Qualified Financing), usually led by an institutional venture capital (VC) fund.
- Sale of the company."[4]

Alec Wright describes these documents as "a little bit more company-friendly and founder-friendly" because they don't call for repayment and interest.

---

[4]https://ca.practicallaw.thomsonreuters.com/w-001-0673(accessed October 31, 2022).

As noted by Alec, the SAFE is considered founder-friendly. It excludes many of the protective provisions included in standard VC preferred-stock agreements. Because of this, you should expect pushback from some investors regarding the use of a SAFE. Other common forms of documentation for issuance of startup-preferred shares are standard NVCA model documents available at: https://nvca.org/model-legal-documents/ and Series Seed docs available at: https://www.seriesseed.com/. Series Seed documents are open-sourced and strive to be simple and avoid legalese.

One common theme to be aware of is that your ownership stake will be subordinated to investors. You and your cofounders and employees will own common stock (or options to buy common stock) and the investors will own preferred stock, which gets paid first in a dissolution (a winding down of the company), should you be acquired, or in a liquidation (a sale of the company's assets). Your attorney will be well versed in all the details of the various options and can advise you which form is best for you.

There are an unlimited number of iterations and nuances associated with structuring venture capital rounds. A good reference for anyone considering a venture equity round is the book and website *Venture Deals: Be Smarter Than Your Lawyer and Venture Capitalist* by Brad Feld and Jason Mendelson (https://www.venture deals.com).

While angels are still reliable sources for the earliest outside funding, there are an increasing number of institutional pre-seed funds that are focused on investing at this stage.

Typically, pre-seed investment would range from $100,000 to maybe $2 million and you should probably give yourself a runway of around a year. While little is expected to be tangible at the beginning of the pre-seed stage, you and your investors should agree on milestones that you hope to achieve during this stage. In fact, this is important at all stages, from pre-seed to growth. Having milestones, such as a minimum viable product at the end of the seed stage, helps you track your progress and gives reassurance to both current and prospective investors.

## Angels

Angel investors are the most common form of financing before institutional money comes in (although, as Alec Wright has pointed out, there are funds, such as his OneValley Ventures, that invest pre-seed). Seed funding was often referred to as the "angel round." Angels will invest in the pre-seed and seed stages.

These investors tend to be people who are not professional investors and are acting in their own capacity rather than as part of a group or fund. According to Alec, the core of angel investing is in the $25,000–$200,000 range, which means the typical size of an individual check falls in that range. That said, there are angels who write checks for as little as $5,000 and as much as $250,000 or more.

Those in the latter group — often called super-angels — might be more knowledgeable and are certainly among the wealthiest of individual investors. It's not uncommon for former founders who have done well to be super-angels. They're motivated by the desire to see another company take off and the possibility of a good return on their investment, as well as a degree of empathy for fellow founders, remembering how daunting raising the first money can be, says Alec.

## Seed

Companies in the seed stage typically have a product in the market and some early revenues. "You want to see product success, traction, and interest from the market," notes Wright. He says that investments in this round typically range from $1.5 million to $3–4 million. In my experience, I've seen them go as high as $10 million.

As with the pre-seed stage, you should raise enough money to last you at least a year, or maybe even 18 months. You'd be surprised how quickly you can go through that money. Consider that you'd probably have five to 10 employees, working for minimal salaries, maybe $100,000 each, as well as some office space.

Seed money can come from a variety of sources: angels and family and friends, but also seed-stage venture funds. You might also hear about "micro VCs." These are small venture funds that focus exclusively on seed-stage investing. Serial startup CEO Dan

Doles says that while raising money is always stressful, it's especially true of the seed round. "They're all stressful in different ways but raising your first round of capital seems like the hardest," he remembers. "You're selling vision and you're selling hope."

This round may be the first one where you take institutional money – money from a professional investor. (It's possible you won't take institutional money until Series A.) What's different about the money you take during the seed stage is that you now have to think about what your board looks like. If a seed investor can contribute value in addition to their capital, you probably want to invite them onto the board. Someone who has lots of startup experience or someone with a strong operating company background may be valuable in helping you avoid mistakes – a priority at this stage.

This is the first stage at which debt is likely to be available to you. If you have raised a year's worth of equity and you can add another six months of runway with debt, you've given yourself six additional months before you have to raise money again, allowing you to achieve more milestones and a higher valuation on your next round. But you need to be confident that you can repay the debt.

If you don't get to where you expected by the time your seed stage is over, you'll probably want to raise a seed-plus round – which is often just an extension of the seed round. It could be that development turned out to be more difficult than you anticipated, or you had to pivot. Having a seed-plus round isn't a huge red flag and shouldn't prevent you from going forward, but it is something that investors will ask about.

## Early Stage

A company in the early stage – Series A and B – is distinguished by several factors. One of the most significant is that from this point on, you take almost exclusively institutional money. The most common source is venture capital, but other potential sources include hedge funds, corporate venture groups, and debt.

For investors to go in on a Series A, they will expect to see a minimum viable product and some early sales traction. If you have an enterprise technology, something you're selling to big businesses, and it's still in beta testing, it will be critical that investors can call some big companies who can vouch for the fact that your product is differentiated and that if the trial goes well, they will become customers.

Once you've gotten your Series A, your likelihood of getting to Series B is very high. There's a good chance your initial investors will have reserved additional capital for the next stage. If you're developing a piece of software or a medical device, and you're six months behind plan, they're very likely to keep funding you.

Ideally, however, in a B round, you will find a new outside lead investor to establish the price and start the march upward in valuation. But to get to that higher valuation, you will have had to accomplish at least some of your Series A milestones and shown that you used the Series A money wisely. Potential investors for a Series B will also look at the management team: How have you built it out? Have you been successful in recruiting and retaining top talent?

Milestones you'd want to hit in Series B include consistently growing revenues month to month. If you're building an app, investors will want to see consistent growth in the user base, even if you're not monetizing it yet. There should be enough data that a trajectory can be seen and some realistic projections made around growth.

Another key distinction from seed to early stage is the composition of your board. Your lead investor for this round will want a seat, and in contrast to the seed stage, at this point the person taking that seat should definitely be adding value. There are things you might give up in order to get a real superstar on your board: you might take a lesser valuation or give up more equity.

Let's say you're looking for $5 million, and one VC offers it in exchange for 20% of the company. Another says, "We need 30% of the company in order to give you $5 million" – but they're offering you someone for the board who can open doors and be a true mentor. It could be worth it to give up more equity if you believe the right board person could help grow your revenues or customer base in a significant way, which will likely pay off in higher valuation for future rounds.

Other terms that might differ include the way the preferences are set, control provisions, and the number of board seats. There are always going to be tradeoffs between what you'd get in a perfect world – high valuation, less dilution, and a marquee name to sit on your board – versus needing the money and not having the luxury of negotiating all the other terms. But to continue to grow, you'll need money.

## Late Stage

Late-stage companies – Series C, D, and beyond – typically have a well-defined business model with attractive unit economics, meaning one that is repeatable and scalable. They usually aren't yet EBITDA-positive, but they have meaningful revenues and a believable path to profitability.

Management should have a clear understanding of how the capital will be used to increase enterprise value. It could be for working capital or to finance an acquisition, but most often it is used to invest in growth. Milestones aren't about technical improvements at this stage but about growth – perhaps 100% revenue growth or launching another product. As Dan Doles points out, during the late stage, your growth trajectory will be the steepest.

## Growth

You're not going to dramatically change your trajectory of growth at this stage. Rather, your goal is to scale the business and that's where the investment goes. Notes Dan Doles, "At this stage, you're typically still investing more than you're making. You could be investing in growing sales and marketing ahead of profitability." The idea is that if you add sufficient sales capacity, you'll increase revenue faster, and eventually you'll cross over to profitability.

"Sometimes, when you really want to accelerate growth, you want to go out and grab market share while the market's hot, and you're probably going to overspend to gain market share, and a lot of times that comes at the expense of profitability," continues Dan. "It certainly comes at the expense of cashflow positivity."

Investing in revenue growth is one aspect of a company in the growth stage. Another is being IPO-ready. If you are on a path to have the profile of a viable IPO candidate, you're probably a growth-stage company. But IPO-ready is a high bar. In normal times, you will need at least $100 million in revenue, growing more than 20% per year, solid margins, a complete management team, a very clear (and near) path to profitability, and, most importantly, a level of predictability to your business that will allow you to provide a growth plan to bankers and investors that you *know* you can achieve. If you have (or soon will have) these attributes, you should pitch growth investors.

In the growth stage, using debt as an alternative to equity can be particularly attractive as a means of minimizing dilution so close to exit or profitability.

There's a specific subset of investors and lenders – called, logically, growth investors and growth lenders – who you can look to at this stage. Here's how working with a growth lender played out with one of our fictional companies:

> Pet food company 19/39 was considering a buyout offer at a key juncture: The company was confident that with more time, it could provide more than anecdotal proof of its key scientific proposition – that nonprescription cat food could make cats produce considerably less allergens. A VC board member, Laura Taitt, suggested that the CEO, Jens Ley, explore venture debt to fund the next stage of the company's growth.
>
> Raising growth capital without the additional ownership dilution and governance strings of more venture capital sounded great to Ley; however, he had never heard of venture debt. Taitt explained that venture debt was a type of loan made to venture-backed companies that are still investing in growth and therefore have yet to reach profitability.
>
> Whereas most lenders shy away from lending to pre-profit borrowers, a small group of specialized funds known as venture lenders are comfortable investing in pre-profit companies by lending against the enterprise value of the business, with the proceeds generally used for important

strategic initiatives. Ley agreed that it sounded like a perfect fit.

Taitt made the case that investing in research and studies to prove Felin' Fine's effectiveness would be the best use of fresh capital. Ultimately, in 2015, 19/39 borrowed $15 million from Pioneer Growth Credit Fund (a fictitious venture-debt lender), avoiding additional dilution.

## Key Takeaways

- Companies are taking institutional money – money from professional investors – later than they used to, with seed money replacing what used to be Series A.
- The stages as used by investors are in reference to funding source, purpose, and sequence.
- Funders and founders should have agreed-upon milestones for each stage.

# Chapter 4

## Geography Matters – to a Point

*For both Nickerson and Ley, CEOs of 4Paws and 19/39 respectively, building their companies in Silicon Valley made sense. They both had strong reputations from their time as early employees at Damascene; they also had vibrant personal and professional networks, which made staffing their companies easier.*

*After Nickerson sold 4Paws, he decided to pursue his animal rights activism as well as using CBD and Kratom for treating diseases in animals. Nickerson moved to Portland, Oregon. The city's emphasis on animal welfare made it a good cultural fit for him, and the fact that the greater Portland area was home to several animal-focused startups meant there would be a pool of talent to draw from for his new company.*

\*\*\*

"Silicon Valley." The name has been synonymous with technology and startups for more than 50 years, and, as discussed in Chapter 6, there is a vibrant ecosystem here supporting entrepreneurs and companies in all stages of growth. Many of the most famous tech startups of the past few decades are headquartered here, and "the Valley," as it is colloquially called, represents about one-third of all venture capital investment, according to CB Insights, amounting to $100 billion in 2021 alone.[1]

While it has some serious rivals – New York City, Boston, and Austin are among the top ones in the United States – Silicon Valley has remained the premier technology hub in this country, if not the world. While there are vibrant tech hubs outside the United States, most notably in China, Israel, and India, as well

---

[1]http://www.bayareaeconomy.org/bay-watch/ (accessed December 27, 2022).

as in parts of Europe, I'll be writing about, and for, startups in the United States, because that's where I've gained my knowledge and experience.

The footprint of the Valley grew along with its influence. The physical area traditionally included the southern part of the San Francisco Bay area (but not the city itself), until recently when the entire Bay Area became considered Silicon Valley. I agree.

## What's in a Name?

Ironically, the name Silicon Valley no longer represents what the businesses here are about. It's a nod to silicon, the critical ingredient in manufacturing semiconductors, and when semiconductor manufacturing dominated the area. Now, many of the big businesses being created here are software related to social, consumer services, and business operations.

But Silicon Valley is more than a place, which is why the moniker carries a certain mystique that belies its geographical boundaries. It's become a term to refer to high-tech businesses in the region, as well as a synonym for the industry overall. As Hollywood is to entertainment, Wall Street is to finance, and Washington, DC, is to government, Silicon Valley is to technology. So when you hear people talk about "Silicon Valley," or "the Valley," figure out the context in which they're using it: the physical location, the industry, or the most prominent companies in the industry.

There was a time when it would have been difficult for me to imagine any serious tech startup being located outside the physical confines of Silicon Valley.

That's no longer the case. "[Being in] Silicon Valley doesn't matter at all anymore," asserts Alec Wright, chief product officer at global entrepreneurial platform OneValley (formerly GSVlabs) and also managing director at early-stage venture fund OneValley Ventures.

With offerings ranging from free software and educational and mentorship programs to a platform that allows communities, government entities, foundations, and other organizations to support entrepreneurship and innovation, OneValley is working to make startup success location-agnostic.

"If you go back 15 years, more than 90 percent of the venture capital that was being deployed, and as a result of that, 90-plus percent of the disruptive technology businesses that were being created, were centralized into a handful of U.S. hubs, starting with Silicon Valley," continues Alec. "If you wanted to launch a company in New Orleans or Boise, it was basically impossible."

Kyle Wong, co-founder and CEO of influencer marketing platform Pixlee TurnTo (now owned by Emplifi), which enables companies to harness the power of user-generated content (UGC), remembers such a time. He started his company in 2010, from an idea born in his Stanford dorm room. "I believe I was very lucky to be in Silicon Valley during that time, because it was the top place to be in tech," says Kyle. "It's definitely a lot less concentrated now, whereas in '09–'10, the startup scene in many U.S. cities was more nascent. You had to go to Silicon Valley to fundraise. And now that's not the case."

## Tiny's Not-So-Small Achievement

Andrew Roberts is one of the founders who did what Alec described as nearly impossible: he built a successful startup, Tiny (Tiny.cloud), about as far away from Silicon Valley as one could get, in Brisbane, Australia.

Tiny, which offers an embeddable rich text editor to a B2B client base, was started in 1999. "An interesting time to start a tech company," Andrew drily acknowledges. "The tech wreck happened shortly after, but I still felt there was this explosion of opportunity that the Internet was creating.

In 2005, Andrew moved to Silicon Valley. "As the business evolved, the market opportunity ended up being about partnering with other software companies and the vast majority of software companies are in the U.S. or headquartered in the U.S.," he says. "We felt that to be competitive we absolutely needed to be in the United States and in the market flying the flag. That was difficult to do from Australia."

In addition to wanting to be near the customer base, the proximity to money was also a key factor behind the move, according to Andrew. "If we ever were to go to the next level, raising capital would be easier in the United States." Access to talent was the third factor. Today, he isn't certain he would feel the same urgency to go to the United States.

He cites a company that started in Poland, which he describes as Tiny's nearest competitor, "as a kind of an A/B experiment." The two companies have almost identical revenue, identical growth rates, and a very similar market. "They're almost a twin from another mother," he says. "They have stayed in Poland, and it doesn't appear to have hurt them very much. It's much more profitable to be able to be based out of there."

Capital, talent, and expertise in such areas as product management and product marketing are now widely available on a global basis. "If you've got a successful business with good traction and good metrics, you can raise money pretty much anywhere," says Andrew. And customers no longer expect companies to be Silicon Valley–based.

At the time of our interview, Tiny was in 22 different countries, with employees widely distributed: there's a marketing person in Canada, an SEO specialist out of Ukraine, a developer in Malta, and large presences in Australia and the Valley. (The company has since been acquired and is now known as TinyMCE.)

Andrew says that if he were to start another company, he would probably do it out of Australia and be fully remote with a mixture of people from all around the world. "The cost advantages of doing that are so much more compelling and now you can tap talent no matter where they are," he says.

Alec Wright points to that lack of infrastructure outside of Silicon Valley, New York, Boston, and Austin designed to accommodate fast-growing companies as the problem. Such companies run on two ingredients: talent and capital.

There are people and organizations like Wright and OneValley who are working to make sure talent and capital are available beyond the physical confines of Silicon Valley. And there are also VC firms and other investing entities intentionally located elsewhere.

One is Research Bridge Partners, which invests both for-profit and not-for-profit money to help encourage commercialization of "mid-continent" medical technology. No less a Valley icon than Reid Hoffman, co-founder of LinkedIn and a partner at Menlo Park–based VC firm Greylock Partners, co-founded Research Bridge Partners. Jim Graham, managing director of investments at Research Bridge Partners, told writer Chris Latham, "Star researchers at leading institutions in the middle of the country often feel they must move to the West Coast or the East Coast to see their ideas become successful ventures. This is a shame, and it hinders the mid-continent's output of successful technology-based startups."[2]

---

[2]https://www.thisiscapitalism.com/venture-philanthropy-research-bridge/ (accessed October 11, 2022).

Steve Case's seed fund, Rise of the Rest, is another proof point that there are high-powered, visible Silicon Valley stalwarts who believe that Silicon Valley doesn't and shouldn't have a monopoly on startups. Mark Kvamme, a prominent VC whose roots were in Sequoia Capital, packed up and moved to Columbus, Ohio, and started Drive Capital.

I don't think it's a case of Silicon Valley becoming less important as much as it is that other places are catching up. The growing importance of what were once secondary hubs or that weren't on the radar 20 years ago hasn't come at the expense of the Big Three. Alec points out the amount of capital that's being deployed in Silicon Valley, New York, and Boston hasn't decreased as money goes to other hubs, established or fledgling, and is being plowed into other places. "If you look at any data that's tracking Silicon Valley, New York, Boston, vs. the world in venture capital, what you'll see is that over the last five to seven years the amount of capital deployed in those markets has either stayed consistent, or actually increased as it did in the 2020 and 2021 boom," he says.

People shouldn't be dissuaded from pursuing their great ideas because of geography. Personally, I believe you can build a great company almost anywhere.

That said, I think there are still some good reasons for a fledgling company to be located here (Silicon Valley). Depending on what stage of maturity your company is at – both in terms of funding and product development – and who your customers are, there's a good chance you'll want some presence here and/or end up doing business here.

The number-1 reason you'd want to be here is that this is where much of the money is – and, as noted earlier, where one third of it is invested. If and when you are looking for investment, ranging from your first seed money to your last round before an exit, you will more than likely be talking to people or firms that are located in the Valley. Those folks might want *you* here. From the VCs' perspective, if they had the choice of flying to Denver to attend a board meeting or just driving a few miles, you know what they'll pick.

One of the reasons that Silicon Valley grew so fast in size, deal velocity, and influence is that there was a time that most VCs had a rule that they wouldn't invest in a company unless they could drive there. They wanted to be able to spend time with the team. Although no longer a hard-and-fast rule, the idea of being able to drive to a meeting was the norm for a very long time. (The people at UC Berkeley – literally 10 miles away, but across a bridge with a lot of traffic – complained that VCs from Silicon Valley wouldn't visit UC Berkeley because it was too far away.)

It's not just investors who will find it more convenient if you're located here, believes Tim Brady, a Stanford grad who was employee number 1 at Yahoo! and was until recently a partner at accelerator Y Combinator. It will be an advantage for you, too. "When you're starting a company and looking for access to people and money, speed is everything. And so if you're elsewhere you have to work just a little bit harder to go meet and find an investor that might want to talk to you," he says. "It might take a week, rather than a day. That's why I think being in Silicon Valley is super-important."

Once companies get beyond the zero-to-20-employee range, their location doesn't matter as much. "Once you get product market fit, and you're growing, and it's pretty clear what your business is, it's less important to be here, because you've already established a handful of relationships, which you can leverage to meet other people," says Tim. "But right at the beginning, it's critical."

Whether you need to be here also depends on what stage your company is at. As Tim says, if you are a later-stage company, the kind Runway Growth lends to, you are likely to have proven already that you are perfectly capable of operating effectively and efficiently in a remote way.

One of the largest single loans we've made is to a company in Houston. Another of our large loans was to a company that not only didn't have an office in Silicon Valley, but didn't have an office, period. When we looked up this company on Google Maps, it turned out that the street view image associated with their address was a storage unit, with the door rolled up. (Yes, you can build a great company anywhere.)

If I were still a VC, would I invest in a startup that wasn't in the Valley? It would depend on a couple of factors. If a team had worked together in the past, and had demonstrated success, then the answer would be yes.

For people who had never worked together, I would be more cautious. The early stage is a very, very stressful time in a startup. It requires 24/7 effort and under these circumstances, it's very easy to have misunderstandings, communication breakdowns, and bruised feelings. When startups fail early on, a common reason is that the founders end up not getting along.

That's why I would be much more comfortable with all the founders being in, let's say, Boulder, than with a team spread all over the country or world, even if one of them lived in Palo Alto.

The concentration of capital, talent, and people who know how to build businesses gives Silicon Valley that X factor – which you can't quite quantify or qualify. "If you walk into a Starbucks in Silicon Valley, you'll see a bunch of other founders pitching investors – that's all anyone's talking about," says Tim. Add in the presence of legendary tech companies, Stanford, and Berkeley, and the history and legacy of the venture money, "it creates something unique."

Brandon Child, a principal at early-stage venture debt company Costella Kirsch, says, "The people here understand the world of technology and capitalization, so there's a serendipitous aspect to being here that I haven't found elsewhere." Brandon benefited from serendipity when he met Costella Kirsch (CK) co-founder Jim Kirsch at his younger brother's baseball game. Kirsch's son was on the same team, which led first to an externship at CK while Brandon was an undergrad and eventually a job after he finished his MBA at UCLA.

Proximity has a power that goes beyond just the physical convenience. You can connect with people via technology, but you *connect* when you're proximal. When there are so many close connections concentrated geographically, things move in a way that even the most sophisticated technology still can't replicate.

"Other than family, that ability to connect was my chief reason for moving back up here. It's not enough to meet someone on a call once and have them *kind of* understand what you're about," says Brandon. "In the world of early-stage companies, finance lending, and getting a referral to someone, it's hard to explain the value of being able to get lunch with someone or go play tennis with them. Once you form a relationship, they understand who you are and that you have integrity."

As Alec Wright says, "There's a density of people who are completely focused on this same goal of building industry-defining technology businesses." He points out that this helps founders "develop relationships and trust with people who can meaningfully transform your company and your future."

There will be new tech hubs, and the current ones will likely continue to thrive – as will Silicon Valley. The more places that are supporting innovation and the more resources there are to help companies grow, the better off everyone is – not just founders and investors, but all stakeholders, including customers.

## Key Takeaways

- Being in Silicon Valley has unique advantages, including concentration of and access to funding, partners, customers, and a wide range of expertise.
- Who your customers are and what stage your company is at will likely influence whether you want to be in Silicon Valley.
- The rise of other tech hubs and the resources to support them isn't at the expense of Silicon Valley.

# Chapter 5

## The Startup Ecosystem

*Silicon Valley is in this never-ending circle. A never-ending circle of this is where our best engineers are. Why? Because that's where companies get started. Why? Because that's where venture capitalists live and they provide funding for those companies. Why are they here? Because the greatest engineers are here. Why? Greatest engineers are here because the companies are here. It's this never-ending Circle of Life in Silicon Valley.*

*–Jan Koum, co-founder and former CEO of WhatsApp[1]*

While Koum's comments are specific to Silicon Valley, he makes an important point about the startup ecosystem overall. It functions because thousands of businesses and service providers are intertwined and interdependent to make the whole greater than the sum of its parts. Even though companies are highly competitive and there are plenty of healthy egos in every corner of the ecosystem, these entities recognize the importance of not only their own role in the ecosystem but those of other members.

Understanding the key components of the ecosystem from a formation and funding perspective will be critical to your success. The more you know, the better equipped you will be to make good choices around how you use your money at all stages.

Key components of the ecosystem include sources of money (everyone from angels and venture capitalists to venture debt lenders and banks), incubators and accelerators that discover, fund, and nurture nascent talent and businesses, academic and

---

[1]https://www.imdb.com/title/tt8128854/ (accessed January 1, 2023).

research facilities, talent of all kinds, and service providers ranging from outsourcing companies to lawyers who specialize in intellectual property.

Not every company will need or use every resource. Perhaps you won't go through an incubator, or you won't ever need to outsource a CFO. And there are others, such as lawyers and accountants, that every company will use.

Rather than list them alphabetically, I've listed them in the order in which you're most likely to need/encounter them. The order won't be perfect; for example, you could end up using venture debt at the early stage, late stage, growth stage, or in all of them. You might return to an incubator or accelerator after receiving external funding.

One reason to stay within the ecosystem whenever possible – that is, to use a lawyer who works with other startups – is that players in the ecosystem know each other and can be very helpful in opening doors for you. Bankers and lawyers know VCs; VCs know venture debt lenders; venture debt lenders know growth equity investors, corporate VCs, and investment bankers.

## How Startup Funding Works

### *Going from Idea to IPO*

# How Startup Funding Works

Going from idea to IPO

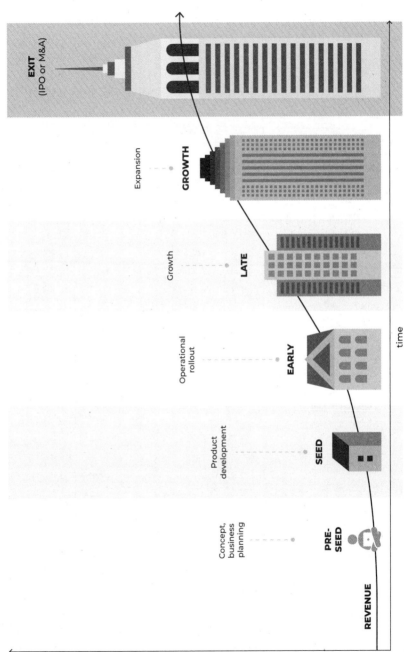

| STAGE | PRE-SEED | SEED | EARLY | LATE | GROWTH |
|---|---|---|---|---|---|
| Source of money | Friends & Family, Personal Savings, Incubators, Public Funding / Grants | Angel Investors, Micro VCs, VCs, Accelerators | VCs, Family Offices, Venture Debt Providers | VCs, Strategics, Venture Debt Providers | Growth Equity Providers, Growth Debt Providers, Bank Debt |
| Purpose of money | Identify and Test Target Market, Develop Product/ Service, Minimum Viable Product (MVP) | Refine Product, R&D, Develop Target Market, Generate Initial Revenues | Execute Go-to-Market Plan, Invest in Sales and Market Share Growth, R&D, Expand Team | Increase Sales Growth, Continued Hiring, Expand Market Opportunity | Demonstrate Path to Profitability and Exit, Complete Team |
| Traction | Customer Validation | Product-Market Fit | Expansion | Significant Scale | Growth & Profitability |
| Product | MVP | Final Testing | Commercially Viable | Fully Scaled | Next Generation / New Product and Segments |
| Team Size | 2-10 | 10-20 | 20-50 | 50-100 | 100+ |
| Duration | 12 to 18 months | 12 to 18 months | 12 to 18 months | 12 to 18 months | 12 to 18 months |
| Ecosystem partners | Attorney, Bank, Incubator | Attorney, Seed Investors, Accelerator | Attorney, VC Investors, Venture Debt Lenders, Go-to-Market Partners, Finance / Ops Service Providers | Attorney, Auditors / Accountants, VC Investors, Venture Debt Lenders, Go-to-Market Partners | Attorney, Auditors / Accountants, Growth Equity Providers, Growth Debt Providers, Investment Bankers |

## *Pre-Seed or Seed Stage*

**Incubators/Accelerators:** At the pre-seed or seed stage – when it's really just you and your idea – you may want to get involved with an incubator and/or accelerator. They're usually run by potential investors and people who serve as consultants, as well as universities and larger companies. They can be especially helpful for first-timers who are unfamiliar with pitching investors.

As the names suggest, incubators help companies get off the ground while accelerators help foster growth, most notably by preparing them to meet with venture capitalists and giving them the opportunity to do so. Some of them are a combination of boot camp and contest, where companies will spend two to six months refining what they're doing, pitching to and getting advice from different people, and then take part in a business-plan competition, with the winner getting funding. The money may be nondilutive or equity.

They're very attractive to fledgling companies – so much so that it's not uncommon for people to do multiple rounds in incubators or accelerators. Even if you don't win money, you'll get a lot of advice. You'll also get introduced into the networks of potential funders, mentors, and other businesses affiliated with the programs.

And sometimes you'll get synergy. You might discover that someone in the same program has an adjacent idea and that it would make sense for you to put your two companies together. An incubator may offer access to additional, valuable resources, such as a lawyer, who you will need sooner rather than later.

Some accelerators or incubators are affiliated in some way with a university. If you developed your product or service through a university's program or one of its labs, you might have to negotiate a license agreement. (An idea hatched in your dorm room, such as Kyle Wong's Pixlee, is different from something that is created or developed with the school's resources.) Every major research university will have a tech transfer office, whose job it is to work out a deal.

For example, Stanford owned part of Google, and the University reaped $336 million from its sale of its stake in Google. The University sold a portion of its shares in Google's IPO, and sold the rest in 2005, a year after the company went public. Harvard made no claim to Facebook even though the idea was born during Mark Zuckerberg's time there because it wasn't sponsored by any university entity.[2]

## OneValley: Doing Well by Doing Good

A classic case of "doing well by doing good" is startup and innovation platform OneValley (formerly known as GSV Labs), which chief product officer Alec Wright calls its own ecosystem. While the organization no longer runs traditional early-stage accelerators and incubators, its online products and services provide acceleration support, much of it free to its community of founders, which exceeds 100,000 entrepreneurs, according to Alec.

The majority of its business, he notes, "is a software-as-a-service platform used by dozens of accelerators and incubators ranging from traditional accelerators to government-funded incubation programs to launch new clean energy technologies and things like that." Alec says, "Over the years, we made the decision to move most of our support resources and activity online, so we weren't limited to the founders that could physically be in our spaces in Silicon Valley, or in Boston, or in Pittsburgh."

Help for pre-seed and seed companies also comes in the form of investment through the OneValley Fund. "The majority of our investments are companies that came into the OneValley ecosystem through one of our online communities or online programs," says Alec. "However, 25% to 30% of our investments are startups we got to know and then post-investment we support them in other ways."

If a portfolio company does a Series A round, the Fund will invest, but it rarely invests beyond Series A, keeping its focus on nascent companies and founders who are starting out. "I think the hidden secret of the startup world is most of the founders that are building and launching early-stage companies don't get the dynamics of the venture-backed startup world," says Alec. "And that's what we're trying to help them with."

**Law Firms:** If you're going to start a company, the first person you will need outside of your actual team is a lawyer. You can go online and establish a legal entity, but an experienced entrepreneur/founder will go to one of the handful of law firms that have expertise in working with startups. Anywhere there is

---

[2]https://www.latimes.com/archives/la-xpm-2005-dec-02-fi-calbriefs2.3-story.html    (accessed January 1, 2023).

even a moderate amount of tech activity, you'll find lawyers with the expertise and connections you are looking for. Some of the top firms include Fenwick & West, Cooley; WSG&R; Gunderson Dettmer Stough; Goodwin Procter; Latham & Watkins; Kirkland & Ellis; Orrick, Herrington & Sutcliffe; Perkins Coie; and DLA Piper.

I highly recommend going to a law firm that has this specific expertise. They tend to be relatively inexpensive for the kind of work you will need early on because they often view doing work like startup documentation as being somewhat of a loss leader. No one ever knows when the next Mark Zuckerberg is walking into their office. Most of the top law firms serving the startup community will attend your board meetings free of charge (it benefits them to be in the room for discussions that may lead to additional legal work).

**Banks:** After you get your legal matters squared away, you'll need to open a bank account. It sounds mundane and obvious, but it's important. In the Valley, there are a number of institutions that call themselves "venture banks" – banks that focus on providing services to venture capital firms and venture-backed startups. Among the top ones are Silicon Valley Bank, CIBC, Bridge Bank, PacWest Bank, Avid Bank, and Comerica Bank. It is wise to use one of these banks because they understand the specific needs of startups.

As your cash balance increases from raising outside capital (debt or equity), you should diversify your banks, so your cash is on deposit with multiple banks or investment firms. This will protect you in the event one of your banks runs into problems.

**Angels:** Angel investors are wealthy private investors who finance small business ventures in exchange for equity. In contrast to venture capital firms, which raise investment funds, angels use their own money. These are often the first outside investors in a company, investing primarily in the pre-seed and seed stages and, in a sense, they are taking the greatest risk. Angels are great for getting started, especially if they bring domain expertise that can help you build your business; however, angels generally don't have sufficient resources to fund you all the way to an exit. You'll most likely need to access the deeper pockets of VC funds beginning with your Series A round.

**Venture Capitalists:** Venture capitalists (VCs) raise money from outside sources, such as large institutional investors (pensions, foundations, endowments, etc.), family offices, and companies, and invest those funds, as well as the firm's money, through funds, which are typically structured as limited partnerships with 10-year lives. The National Venture Capital Association (NVCA) estimates that there are approximately 5,400 U.S.-based venture capital funds managed by approximately 3,000 venture capital firms. As of 2021, NVCA estimates that 84% of U.S. VC capital was managed in three states: California, Massachusetts, and New York.

**Venture Debt Lenders:** In contrast to venture capital investors, who take equity, venture debt lenders are a source of funding that involves a loan (versus an equity investment), which results in minimal dilution of equity. That is a big advantage to founders, VCs, and others with a financial stake who have an interest in keeping equity from being further diluted.

Venture debt can be taken at any stage, but it's most common in the late and growth stages, when companies are more mature and confident in their ability to repay loans. In Part Three, I'll provide more details and insights on the pros and cons of debt versus equity.

## Outsourcers and Recruiters

Whether you're looking for part-time coders or developers, product designers, or a consultant to work in a senior-level position, such as someone to serve as a chief financial officer, there are businesses that specialize in supplying these resources. Think of them as outsourcers, although they most likely will call themselves something else.

It's worth mentioning that outsourcing of coding and development is often done to other parts of the world and that can be risky. As I was writing this book, Russia had invaded Ukraine – a major hub for outsourced technology work. One of my portfolio companies' entire development team was based in Kharkiv. They moved as many people as possible to Poland and other more hospitable European countries. Other employees remained to fight by day and code by night.

While still in the startup phase you definitely should be out-sourcing functions like PR and branding, and possibly HR. It's not capital-efficient to have many of these functions in-house. Commonly used outsourcers for HR services are TriNet and Insperity.

**IP Lawyers:** Most major law firms have intellectual property attorneys, but in my experience, founders tend to go with bou-tique, specialized firms. Generally speaking, the best IP attorneys are steeped in the relevant technology and engineering, and they tend to congregate in smaller, specialized firms.

You might not need an IP lawyer when you first start the legal documentation for your company – which you will recall I recom-mend that you do just about at the start of your business – but you *will* need an IP lawyer when you have intellectual property that you intend to protect with a patent.

## Protecting Your IP

Before you speak publicly about your technology, be certain the patent will be protected regarding a "prior art" claim. All of this is somewhat arcane, but below are some basics, borrowed from U.S. government sites. Obviously, this is not meant to serve as or be a substitute for legal advice.

According to the United States Patent and Trademark Office (USPTO),

> Prior art constitutes those references or documents which may be used to de-termine novelty and/or non-obviousness of claimed subject matter in a patent application.[3]
> Common types of prior art include:

Printed Documents

Patents and published patent application (domestic and foreign)

Non-Patent Literature: magazine articles, newspaper articles, electronic publica-tions, online databases, websites, or Internet publications (MPEP 2126-2128).

"Otherwise available to the public" is a new catch-all provision of 102(a)(1) that has no explicit counterpart in pre-AIA law.[4]

---

[3]https://www.uspto.gov/sites/default/files/documents/May%20Info%20Chat%20slides%20%28003%29.pdf (accessed August 18, 2022).

[4]https://www.uspto.gov/patents/laws/america-invents-act-aia/america-invents-act-aia-frequently-asked (accessed September 20, 2022).

For example:

- an oral presentation at a scientific meeting
- a demonstration at a trade show
- a lecture or speech
- a statement made on a radio talk show
- a YouTube video, website, or other online material (this type of disclosure may also qualify as a printed publication under AIA [America Invents Act] and pre-AIA law).

What does this mean for you? Don't talk, tweet, make a TikTok, or post ANY kind of reference anywhere (outside your company) regarding something you want to patent. It could be a breakthrough technology worth big money. You want to protect that.

A small but critical piece of intellectual property that Amazon patented was one-click purchasing. Prior to the patent's expiration in 2017, Amazon made billions by licensing it to other online companies, including Apple.[5]

**Accounting Firms:** From the very beginning you will need to be able to keep accurate books and records. Having a qualified, experienced financial person (internal or outsourced) appropriate for your company's stage is mandatory. (See Chapter 15 for thoughts on when and how to add this resource.) Most early-stage, venture-backed companies are not audited. Since the VCs generally have complete access to all the information they desire, they don't feel that the cost of a full audit is worth it. Startups normally won't get a full audit until they're forced to, with the forcing function often being taking a meaningful loan from a bank or nonbank lender like Runway Growth Capital. Most lenders require that their borrowers receive annual audit reports from a credible accounting firm.

That said, we're not going to require an audit from one of the Big Four accounting firms. And you don't need one of that size even in anticipation of going public. An audit from a tier 2 firm should suffice. Go to a firm that has expertise in doing audits of companies of your general size and composition.

---

[5]https://digiday.com/marketing/end-era-amazons-one-click-buying-patent-finally-expires/ (accessed August 18, 2022).

As with lawyers, accountants are hoping that they're auditing the next Meta, so they price these services at a rate where they're likely going to lose money for the first few years, expecting that they can make up for it if there's an IPO or an M&A transaction.

**409A Valuations:** These are a critical bit of financial housekeeping that you'll want to have an expert perform for you. According to information resource Holloway:

> A 409A valuation is an assessment private companies are required by the IRS to conduct regarding the value of any equity the company issues or offers to employees. A company wants the 409A to be low, so that employees make more off options, but not so low the IRS won't consider it reasonable. In order to minimize the risk that a 409A valuation is manipulated to the benefit of the company, companies hire independent firms to perform 409A valuations, typically annually or after events like fundraising.[6]

This is not the equivalent of an audit. It's a valuation of equity for purposes of stock options and is designed to protect the recipient of those options from being deemed later to have been granted what they call "cheap stock" and then being taxed on it down the line.

**Insurers; D&O Insurance:** Insurance involves everything from health insurance for your employees to protecting directors and officers (D&O) in the event of a lawsuit. Don't skimp on this or wait to get it. Having the proper insurance to protect your key people in the event of a lawsuit will enhance your ability to attract employees and board members and will be critical to your ability to raise money. Most VCs and many angels won't sit on a board unless the company has adequate D&O insurance.

**Private Equity Investors:** Private equity (PE) plays an important role in the startup ecosystem as a frequent buyer of venture-backed businesses. PE participation in growth rounds is small but growing. PE investors generally have a different business model and ethos than VC firms. PE tends to buy established businesses

---

[6]https://www.holloway.com/definitions/409a-valuation (accessed December 27, 2022).

that need shoring up so the businesses can then be sold for a higher valuation; venture capital is focused on helping startups grow. PE firms are constantly looking for acquisitions that they can "bolt on" to an existing "platform" company they already own. The startup ecosystem has become an important source of bolt-on acquisitions for PE-owned companies.

## Key Takeaways

- Your need for different parts of the ecosystem will largely depend on which stage you are in.
- Some needs will be constant – lawyers, for example – while you may never use other parts, such as an outsourcer.
- Whenever possible, use service providers who have expertise with startups.

# Part Three

## Getting the Money

# Chapter 6

## Your First Outside Investors

"The tech world is crazy," says Kyle Wong, CEO and co-founder of Pixlee TurnTo. "Think of it logically. It's wild that people would give 22-year-olds right out of college millions of dollars to test very unproven ideas."

He has a point. That said, I wish it were true that everyone who has a great, scalable idea for a business, whether it's going to affect billions of people on the planet, such as Google, or be a more niche player, like SaaS billing automation platform Aria Systems, gets the money they need.

"There are a lot of very practical challenges that every fledgling company faces, and funding is only one of them, but funding is essential to all of it," says Alec Wright. "You have to recruit and convince people to join your venture and get people who have the skills you need excited about your brand-new idea that's likely unfunded, and you're not able to pay them anywhere near what they're making in their current roles."

The number of businesses that succeed and flourish indicates that many deserving companies do of course get funded. Statistics are quickly outdated, but if you're looking for current ones, check the quarterly report from the National Venture Capital Association (NCVA) and Pitchbook. Even with pullbacks in funding, which we were seeing in 2022 as I was writing this book, there is still plenty of money flowing into Silicon Valley, and there are VC firms and lenders with significant dry powder, although this could change quickly if the ultimate suppliers of capital to the ecosystem (large institutions like pensions, foundations, and endowments) slow down their commitments to venture capital and venture debt funds.

Whatever trends are prevailing at the time you're looking for funding may have as much to do with current affairs, politics, public stock prices, or other macro factors as with the validity of the idea. When money and attention flow to certain sectors or solutions, it could lead you to think that only certain types of businesses get funded. While certain sectors do go in and out of favor, this doesn't mean your idea has to fall within the current "hot" sector to get funding. The VC model itself, with a small percentage of the investments returning the majority of the profits, shows that the wrong bets are often made. (We use "bets" and "investments" interchangeably.)

There are probably few things as painful for a founder as seeing a company get funding when yours didn't – and then seeing that company fail. You can't help but think that you would have made better use of that money or been a better bet. As many companies that fail to make it past the early stage, there are even more that don't get beyond seed funding – if that far.

Taking funding out of the equation, it's not always clear why some companies make it and others don't. It's usually not for lack of hard work. Says Alec, "Sometimes you just can't get it to hit and it's hard watching people putting in 150% day after day and do the right things, but they still didn't achieve what they needed to."

On the other hand, he says, there are a lot of people launching businesses who just don't get the playbook or have unrealistic expectations of what input is needed to generate the output they want. "Those 'come to Jesus' conversations are often challenging, because you have to say, 'I know you're excited about this and I know you're working really hard on this. But if you stay on the current trajectory, it's highly likely that this just isn't going to go anywhere."

## Eye of the Investor

When it comes to funding companies, beauty is in the eye of the investor – and not every investor has the same eye. There are highly successful companies that got passed on by one or more

VCs that went on to make a fortune for those who invested in them. It's not always clear why a startup that looked like a stinker to one VC looked like a winner to another. Even the best firms and their top VCs have missed out on great investments. For example, Kleiner Perkins' John Doerr, a legendary VC who invested early in such winners as Google and Amazon, passed on Tesla.

A company gets funded because somebody (or more than one person) believes that it has the potential to be a scalable and profitable business. You don't have to be successful – yet – to get your initial money. Early investors are betting on potential more than proof. Don't get me wrong, proof (or traction, in VC parlance) is always good, but at the earliest stages, you will be selling yourself and your vision.

One of the most basic and critical things you can do to appeal to an investor – or lender – at any stage is to have a professional presentation. Make it thorough (but succinct), accurate, easy to read, and understandable. Your presentation should be no more than a dozen pages. If needed, you can include additional information in an appendix. If you can't sum up your idea in a compelling way in 10 or 12 slides, you're not ready to ask anyone for money (even your parents). It may seem like overkill, but you should, from the very beginning, create a fully functioning, three-statement, completely linked financial model that allows you and potential investors or lenders to do scenario analysis. It shows that you understand the metrics that drive your business and will serve you well as you consider various paths, pivots, and growth alternatives.

Kyle says that demonstrating focus is key. "One of the most important things that often gets overlooked in company building is the concept of focus and having expertise in a certain area, because you're not going to have the breadth of a company with tens of thousands of employees working on thousands of product lines," he says.

But it takes more than a solid presentation and focus to secure money. Let's assume a few things: you're beyond asking family and friends, and you don't have any kind of track record or reputation, or even a co-founder who is a superstar engineer. How do you get that pre-seed or seed money? The first place to start is angel networks. Almost every big city has at least one angel club; many cities have multiple ones.

Look for an angel or a wealthy, successful individual who, ideally, has made money in the space in which you want to build a business. Their knowledge of the space will be an advantage to you both. While they are obviously motivated by the idea of financial return, such people often find it appealing and satisfying to help an entrepreneur and an early-stage idea blossom.

There are also institutional seed funds, such as Ulu, run by Miriam Rivera and Clint Korver, and Pear.vc, founded by Pejman Cozad and Mar Hershenson. Again, look for those who have made investments in your space. That's where you're likely going to have the most success.

Whether or not you're successful in finding a fit with one or more angel investors, you should also consider an incubator or accelerator.

Incubators help startup entrepreneurs refine their ideas and build their company from the ground up. Accelerators provide early-stage companies that already have an MVP (minimum viable product) with the education, resources, and mentorship needed to develop in several months what might otherwise take years to accomplish.

As I discussed in Chapter 5, "The Startup Ecosystem," incubators and accelerators can be a huge help in terms of opening doors and getting your name and idea known.

If you've gotten the backing of credible angels, that will be a huge help when you are looking for institutional money, especially your Series A round. Existing investors are the best source of introductions to new investors. In addition, your law firm – which you should be engaging with early on – will be another important source of good introductions. Some VCs say they won't even look at companies that don't come with an introduction.

VCs will often pick an industry they want to specialize in, and venture-backed companies – or those looking to be venture-backed – ideally want to attract knowledgeable capital. Your first lead investor will take a board seat, and ideally you want someone with knowledge about your space. Larger firms might have a research team whose job it will be to identify the most interesting and/or promising companies in their area of interest.

That's why you need to do everything you can to raise your profile so you'll be easier to find. That means not only maximizing the use of social media, but taking advantage of networking opportunities – everything from formal ones such as industry conferences to being part of the community in some way. As a founder of a fledgling company, you're not likely to have time for volunteer work, so you should consider taking advantage of other opportunities to meet people.

With regard to early-stage debt (something Runway does not do; we lend to late- and growth-stage companies), venture banks and nonbank lenders are directly approachable or easily accessed via an introduction from your equity investors, attorneys, or advisors. Brandon Child, a managing director at early-stage lender Costella Kirsch, says he values the introductions that come to his firm from a trusted source.

"For someone to want to bring you in and say, 'Hey, this is a guy you should work with, they need to get to know you,' says a lot, because it's their personal capital at stake," says Brandon. "There are a lot of ways that you can play tricks in business, and in Silicon Valley, because it's a small ecosystem, people are generally trying to be good operators, because their reputation is more important than any single profit or any single deal." Brandon's point about reputation, while true about the Valley, certainly holds true throughout the startup community and beyond. (See more about the importance of reputation in Chapters 13 and 14.)

The big issue we haven't talked about is who doesn't get the money – and who historically hasn't. It's no secret that for many years, Silicon Valley and other tech hubs in the United States have been dominated by men – and largely white men – in terms of both founders and financers. That's changing, of course, as well it should.

Whatever disadvantages you may have had to fight, what you look like, what pronouns you use, where you are from, your gender or orientation, shouldn't be a deterrent. Everyone has the right to seek funding – investments, loans, grants, and so on – and should have equal opportunity to do so. Everyone. That's been a guiding principle of mine not only at Runway but throughout my career. No one should believe they haven't got a chance because of a circumstance they couldn't control.

We know it hasn't worked out that way. This isn't a topic I'm going to belabor, and not because I don't think it's important or because I don't care. My purpose is to help you understand the different sources and types of money, the implications of each type of money, and how to use that money wisely and well.

## Who Doesn't Get the Money

Ulu Ventures, co-founded by spouses Clint Korver and Miriam Rivera, is looking to increase the amount of seed-stage funding that goes to diverse founders and their companies.

"Our view is that talent is equally distributed, but opportunity is not," says Clint, managing director at the firm. "If we can create opportunities for diverse entrepreneurs who, by the way, aren't getting funded other places, we should generate superior returns."

That's not to say that Ulu will invest in any and every company with a female or minority founder. Those superior returns aren't by accident. Clint, who has founded several companies, describes his background as one rooted in "decision making under uncertainty."

Venture capital, he points out, is an entire industry focused on making decisions. "From my point of view, you can actually be systematic about evaluating risk and return. There are a whole bunch of analytic tools you could apply to venture just like every other financial asset has done over the last couple of decades." Venture capital is "behind the times" relative to public equities and quant hedge funds, he says.

Ultimately, Ulu's goal is to change the industry in two ways: by increasing the capital that goes to women and minorities, and by generating better returns than the industry average. "If we can demonstrate that we're getting outsize returns with our investments in under-represented founders, it proves both the validity of our quantitative approach, and that diverse investments can be smart ones." The idea is not to show causality; just the opposite. Ultimately, he says, Ulu wants to be agnostic about its investments, welcoming all kinds of entrepreneurs.

"We make all of our decisions based on a probability-weighted multiple on invested capital," says Clint. "A lot of VCs will say, 'If I invest in a company, I want a 10× return.' We say the same thing, but it is probability weighted. And so we've got a process where we take things like team risk, customer risk, and competition and literally turn it into an Excel spreadsheet model." According to Clint, running an uncertainty analysis allows Ulu to calculate the probability-weighted multiple and make better assessments around valuation and pricing.

"We've got a very principled approach to pricing," continues Clint. "Almost everybody else in the industry, when you ask, 'How did you come up with a price on it?' they'll say, 'The last company I invested in looked just like yours and I gave them a $20 million valuation, so I'm giving you a $20 million valuation." Clint says once Ulu is done creating a model, they give it to the entrepreneurs.

Without a systematic decision-making process, biases can show up, many of which will be unconscious, he believes. "Having a rigorous way of quantifying risk and laying out your decisions allows you to counteract your biases," he says. "Much of the work we do around decision making and diversity we make available to the entire industry, and I know of about a half dozen venture firms that are trying to replicate Ulu's decision process, and we're happy to help them do that."

Of course, you have to get the money, and if you're a CEO and you're putting together your team, diversity matters. People at all levels and in all parts of the ecosystem are looking to see historically underrepresented groups become more prominent. At Runway, now that we are publicly traded, we have to report the makeup of our board to NASDAQ. By 2024, we will be required to have at least one woman on our board. We're lucky that we already have Julie Persily, a rock star, on our board.

I can say this with confidence: even with the pullbacks in funding we saw starting in 2022 as I was writing this book, there was still a lot of institutional money going toward investors who focus on female and minority entrepreneurs. But if you look at the VC community, something like 60% went to Harvard or Stanford, and 95% are white men. It's just staggeringly homogeneous and nondiverse. The pool of entrepreneurs is much more diverse, and changing, but it's still not that representative of what our country looks like.

I'm confident that we'll see more diversity throughout the startup ecosystem going forward, but progress won't be as quick as most of us would like.

## Key Takeaways

- Referrals are critical to getting money at each step and to advancing to the next step.
- Networking is key to increasing your chances of getting funded.
- Efforts are being made to address the lack of diversity throughout the ecosystem.

# Chapter 7

## What Kind of Money Is Right for Your Business?

The kind of money you take for your business will depend on a combination of factors. The most critical ones are the stage your company is at; whether you have revenue and what kind it is; how confident you are in your ability to project your future financial results; your relationships with your existing investors/lenders; and how well you understand the implications of taking on debt versus giving up ownership in exchange for equity.

There isn't a right answer; nor does it have to be either/or. Many companies, even in the early stages, find that a combination of equity and debt – sometimes taken together, sometimes not – is the optimal solution.

Retaining equity isn't a matter of concern only for founders. Even the most junior people at a startup will be attuned to the equity they get and what it's potentially worth. If you can get the growth capital you need without giving up equity, that means more potential value for your team, and that can be a big morale boost and makes your startup more attractive than another.

After the seed stage, your options for putting new money that isn't your own into your business basically come down to taking on VC money or taking on debt. VC money always comes in exchange for equity, but it doesn't incur any fixed financial repayment obligation on your part. Debt, whether from the Small Business Administration, a bank, or a venture lender, comes with the expectation that the money will be paid back.

If debt is not repaid, lenders will typically have alternative paths to recover their investment. The paths available to lenders will differ depending on the source of the loan. SBA and bank loans normally require personal guarantees. Although venture debt typically does not require a personal guarantee, an unresolved payment default on venture debt can result in a sale of your company on a time frame that's out of your control and may not maximize value.

"I think of outside money as being on a spectrum," says Brandon Child, a founder of Sir Kensington condiments (now owned by Unilever), and a managing director at early-stage venture lender Costella Kirsch. "There's equity, which is the most flexible form of capital a company can raise because it's generally unrestricted and it doesn't have to be repaid. Then, on the other end is bank debt. And banks are generally the most restricted if things aren't going well in the business, the availability of that capital may be restricted, and you have to pay it back. But it's usually the least expensive form of debt. And then in the middle is venture debt."

Venture debt is a loan that you take as an alternative or complement to equity capital. It's most commonly used for working capital in growing companies, that is, to fund operations and meet short-term obligations. In addition to enabling companies to accelerate their growth without equity dilution, venture debt can extend a company's runway. That means giving the startup more time between raising additional rounds of venture capital or reducing the number of rounds it might need.

The question of what kind of money is right for your business is central to the thesis of this book (and its title): not all money is created equal. VC money doesn't have to be paid back. That doesn't mean that the money is without cost to you. In exchange for an investment, you give up equity – ownership in the company. Debt has to be paid back, but it allows you to keep a larger percentage of your business.

## Convertible Notes/Convertible Debt

Convertible notes/convertible debt (they refer to the same type of financing) are loans made generally by equity investors with an expectation that they will NOT be repaid but will instead convert into equity. Convertible debt is really an "equity first" instrument, while venture debt is a "debt first" instrument (meaning the lender expects to be repaid and is not making the investment in anticipation that the loan will convert to equity).

This instrument is very often used in seed and other rounds that may take some time to get fully funded so the company can access some of the proceeds before the entire round is raised. These notes may also include a discount on the new round price upon conversion to incentivize investors to participate early.

The "note" explains the details of the debt. It will include such information as when the loan matures, what the balance will be, and what the interest rate/total amount of interest due is. The loan is not paid off along the way but at the maturity date. The presumed and preferred form of repayment is in the form of equity, and this repayment normally is done at the same time as an additional round of funding.

Just as lenders expect to be paid back (I assure you that I prefer being paid back to owning the assets of a liquidated company), convertible note investors expect to be paid back in equity. They are making the loan on the assumption that the company will be valuable enough for equity to make sense for both parties.

The ownership (who owns what percentage) and the preference stack (the order in which people get to "cash in" their stake) matter in the event of an exit. It's worth noting that both debt and preferred equity (typically owned by VCs) sit above the entrepreneur (who typically owns common stock), meaning you will get your money after lenders are paid back and after VCs redeem or convert their preferred stock.

A combination of debt and equity can give you flexibility, points out Kyle Wong. "One of the most important things is to have optionality, whether it's different VCs that you have lined up who want to invest in you, whether it's other funding options, like venture debt, or whether it's just running the business as is without any funding," he says. "That's one of the most important parts of a fundraising process: to drive urgency but ultimately having multiple options around the table."

"As a founder, I'm not saying that venture debt is for everyone," he continues. "It's a great option to have around the table to either extend your existing round, or instead of doing a round."

The secret of raising capital, says Ulu's Clint Korver, is raising just enough money to get to the next stage. "Companies don't raise all the money they need to go public upfront because it's too risky and therefore too expensive," he says. "I would argue one of the biggest challenges for an entrepreneur when it comes to capital is, how do you bring in the cheapest amount of capital possible, but enough of it to get you to the next stage and the next round of capital."

Clint estimates that approximately 20% of Ulu's companies raise debt in the early stages. "Venture debt essentially helps you play the game in a smarter way," he says. "Our companies raise venture debt to extend their runway a little bit, hopefully take some more risk off the table."

## When to Borrow Money

Kyle says the ideal time is when you have found a repeatable business model. By then, you will have no problem attracting additional venture capital – but why give up the dilution if you can avoid it? "Once you feel like you have found that model, venture debt and different funding amounts and sources become very handy to have in place."

That said, don't necessarily go for the lowest interest rate. Go for the best partner – a fund/firm or bank that has a good reputation and wants to create a relationship, not just do a transaction. That means asking for referrals, checking around, taking the measure of the people you're negotiating with. And of course, you have to decide whether to use a bank or a venture debt lender.

### A Spoon versus a Fork

One needs to be confident to use debt, observes Jack Harding, CEO of eSilicon. "When people always ask me, 'When don't you use debt?' my answer almost always is 'When you're not confident in your own business,'" says Jack. He's right. If you can't service debt, having it hanging around your neck is extremely burdensome.

> Both VCs and entrepreneurs are universally confident, optimistic people, notes Jack. "In particular, entrepreneurs think they're headed to the moon," he says. "On the other hand, VCs usually have a touch of pragmatism to them, and a certain degree of self-interest."
>
> He points out that VCs often argue that "All money is green," meaning it's all the same. "That couldn't be further from the truth," asserts Jack. "There are often onerous terms and conditions that are foisted upon novice CEOs who don't realize that they're giving up way too much of their company. And once they realize it, they really can't do anything about it."
>
> That's why he is a proponent of using both equity and debt. "Equity has its place, just as venture debt lenders do," he says. "Sometimes you want to use a spoon; sometimes you want to use a fork. But you have to know when and how to use each."

The biggest demarcation between venture lenders – regardless of whether they're an early-stage lender, like Costella Kirsch, or a growth lender, lending to late- and growth-stage companies, like Runway – and the majority of the lending world is we largely lend to companies that are not yet profitable or cash-flow-positive. That cuts out 99.9% of lenders. Saying "not yet profitable" versus "not profitable" is a distinction *with* a difference. We're only going to lend to companies that we feel confident will become profitable.

## Banks versus Venture Debt Lenders

In addition to there being companies like Runway Growth Capital that only issue venture debt, there are banks that specialize in making loans to venture-backed companies. The difference is we think of ourselves as "growth" lenders, while banks are more likely than we would be to lend to companies that aren't yet on a strong growth trajectory.

Banks can be phenomenal partners and they play an important role in the ecosystem, and they should be considered, but there are pros and cons to taking a bank loan. Banks are federally regulated, so they have less latitude to structure deals in ways that might lend themselves to the needs of a startup. And there could be a situation beyond a bank's control where they suddenly have to call (demand repayment on) a loan.

Whether a bank makes sense as your lender depends on a couple of things. One of them is how much money you need. A bank would likely lend only 5% of your enterprise value. If that's all you need, a bank is a great option, because their interest rate will likely be cheaper than a venture debt lender, points out Armentum's Hutch Corbett, whose firm specializes in helping venture-backed companies raise debt.

A bank can be a good fit under certain circumstances. If a bank isn't the right choice, it doesn't mean that every or any venture debt lender will do. In addition to distinctions around reputation and philosophy – ours is about being a partner, not merely a party to a transaction – there are also different ideas about what kind of clients a venture debt lender wants.

Runway Growth is not the lender for everyone. We don't do anything in the real estate space, for example. It's probably the most lent-to industry in the world, and because it's so well-served we really can't add – or earn – any value.

Our model also doesn't look to lend money to startups that are real-estate-intensive businesses. For example, according to IBIS*World*, the blow-dry salon market was valued at $11.3 billion in December 2021, having experienced annual growth of 7.5% from 2016 to 2021. Not a small market and not bad growth.[1]

But it's mostly a real-estate-based business. Unless the hair stylist is going to a customer's home, the blow-dry business is about salons, and physical infrastructure. That usually means leases, and leases represent a fixed cost that needs to be paid regardless of whether or not the salon is producing revenue (or profit). Large, fixed cost commitments impede the borrower's flexibility in reducing costs in the event of declining revenues (perhaps in a recession). For this reason, we generally avoid businesses with brick-and-mortar footprints, although we do make some exceptions for omni-channel businesses whose roots are in e-commerce.

But that's *our* model at Runway Growth. We're not the only venture debt lender. If you've got a proven business model and a growing business, the chances are that there is a partner for you out there.

---

[1]https://www.ibisworld.com/united-states/market-research-reports/blow-dry-bars-industry/ (accessed May 21, 2022).

## How Equity and Debt Helped Enable a Pivot

Mojix, a global leader in item-level intelligence solutions for manufacturing, supply chain, and retail, started off as primarily a hardware business some 10 years before Dan Doles joined as CEO. He found a mixed bag at best. As Dan recalls the situation, the hardware business wasn't working, but the company had a plethora of intellectual property – close to 100 patents.

Despite having raised five or six rounds of equity, including with one of the larger venture capital firms, the company needed capital, including a new lead investor. The board recommended raising debt instead of equity and became one of Runway Capital's first portfolio companies.

Prior to Dan joining, the company had been developing a software platform as a complement to the hardware. "You couldn't use the hardware without the software. Originally, the plan was to use independent software vendors that we would integrate to and feed data to from the hardware system," says Dan. "That was just too hard. The customers were really looking for someone to provide both." Right before Dan joined Mojix, the company had begun working with a development team in Bolivia that Dan had used in the past.

Dan soon realized that the hardware business was in far worse shape than he had been led to believe, mostly because of market-related reasons. "It was clear to me from the beginning that we needed to make a pivot to software," he says. The largest investor wanted to continue to fund the company to focus on hardware, but as Dan had anticipated, raising another round proved difficult.

"We hired an investment banker and we shopped the hardware business around, and we shopped the whole business around for investment," he says. "No one wanted a company that was sort of half-software, half-hardware. Most investors were looking for a simplified business model – either you're all software or you're all hardware." With no interest in the hardware business and its niche product, Dan intensified his effort to pivot the company to software.

"I went to the board and said, 'Look, we need to just focus on building an SaaS business. And, by the way, I'm going to need more money to do that.' It was such a fundamental pivot from the original investment thesis that the investors didn't want to do it.

"Runway put together a term sheet calling for it to provide additional debt as well as for current investors to put in additional equity. When they weren't willing to participate, David [Spreng] ended up in a position where he had put a lot of debt into the business, in addition to owning the majority of the equity when everyone else failed to participate."

Dan says that doing a pivot right before COVID was less than ideal timing. Still, the more challenging part was getting the capital needed to execute, which turned out to be a combination of debt and equity – simultaneously.

## When Debt Doesn't Make Sense

After you raise your Series A, we usually advise companies to raise some debt in every subsequent funding round. "Venture debt was recommended by our investors as a natural thing to do when you raise a Series A and Series B," says Kyle Wong. However, there are times it doesn't make sense to take on debt, even though that will mean more dilution than a mix of venture equity and venture debt would.

Exceptions to taking on debt with an investment round include when you can't confidently predict revenues and/or expenses; or when you can already see that the business plan will require a large amount of additional funding in subsequent years and existing investors can't or won't commit their financial support.

Another circumstance when borrowing money doesn't make sense is when the payoff schedule will be too aggressive, meaning you will likely end up in violation of your covenants. This can happen when you have a perfectly sound product or offering but its development and launch take longer than expected. Unless you are really confident that you can repay or refinance the debt, raise equity or sell some part of the business. Venture debt is for when you *can* raise equity but choose not to.


## On the Fence

There are times when it isn't clear how best to balance the desire to minimize dilution and the wish to remain debt-free. And it won't always be your choice. I recall discussing a potential loan with a company that had raised its Series B and was developing a new product that its VCs believed could be revolutionary. Although the product was still in the very early stages, the VCs were swinging for the fences, looking to invest as much as possible.

With a possible blockbuster on the horizon, they were eager to increase their ownership stake and insisted that the Series C not be complemented with any venture debt. Consequently, in the Series C, with no venture debt as part of the funding mix, the founders' equity stake was reduced from 45% to 21%.

It's understandable why the management team would go along with an all-equity raise and accept so much additional dilution because had the product been the anticipated game-changer, the company's overall valuation would have increased exponentially. Would you rather own 45% of a company worth $100 million, or 21% of a company worth $2 billion?

It turns out the product being developed wasn't the "next big thing." The VCs didn't see a dime on that investment. It turns out that it was fortunate for both Runway and the founders not to have taken on debt. (That said, I'm not sure that we ultimately would have lent them the money. We had not yet done our due diligence on the company.) The funding eventually dried up, as did the company.

Andrew Roberts, founder and CEO of Tiny (now TinyMCE) points out that sometimes not taking any money – equity or debt – is optimal. "Bootstrapping sounds really dire, but ideally you make money on your customers – we call that customer finance," he says. "Just because you're not raising outside money doesn't mean that you're scraping by."

A decades-long licensing agreement with IBM was pivotal to Tiny's success, funding a significant amount of research and development. "We raised far more money from IBM, like licensing our technology, than we ever did from a venture capitalist." Nondilutive partnership capital can be ideal if it doesn't require tangential technological development that forces a loss of focus on the core mission.

Creative "customer finance" structures are always worth exploring. Something as simple as a prepaid invoice can help with cash flow. Joint development efforts, joint ventures, licensing agreements, and many other arrangements can result in nondilutive funding from your customers. Just be mindful not to sell the company without getting paid for it (by becoming overly beholden to one customer/partner to the detriment of overall value creation).

If structured correctly, you can make your technology/solution so engrained in your partners' business that they need to buy you. Another complication (or potential benefit) is that, today, most large tech companies have internal corporate VC arms that will likely want to invest in you in connection with strategic relationship.

## Key Takeways

- After the seed stage, additional capital will come almost exclusively in the forms of venture capital or venture debt.
- Choosing between venture debt and venture capital will affect how much equity you keep in your startup.
- The choice between venture debt and venture capital may not be yours. Just as you may look to minimize dilution, investors will likely want to increase their stake.

# Chapter 8

# The Ins and Outs of Venture Capital

If you are already familiar with how venture capital, venture capitalists, and venture capital funds work, feel free to skip this chapter. On the other hand, if the specifics are still somewhat murky to you, this chapter – done largely in a question-and-answer format – should give you enough knowledge to feel informed and confident when talking to a VC and making decisions.

There are numerous books and online resources around venture capital. The information here is not intended to be a substitute for a deep dive into the subject or for performing your own due diligence on specific VCs or venture capital firms.

## How is venture capital different from angel money?

VC money is institutional money – money that is invested by firms that are full-time, professional investors. Angels are individuals investing their personal capital.

## What is the difference between venture capital and private equity?

While venture capital is technically a form of private equity – both VC firms and PE firms invest in nonpublic companies – the goals are different. VC firms take minority stakes in growing companies in which the investment is used to fund losses in support of further growth; private equity is investing with an eye toward either owning the company outright or at least having a majority stake. PE investments are almost always used to facilitate the acquisition of a profitable company.

## Where does the money for venture capital come from?

A venture capital firm – for the sake of this chapter, we'll call it Tempus Fugit – will seek investors to amass a pool of money of a specific amount. (To the best of my knowledge, no venture capital firm of that name exists.)

Investors in venture capital funds are generally large institutional investors: state government pension funds, corporate investment funds, insurance companies, family offices, university endowments, wealthy families, foundations, and certain intermediaries (consultants, funds of funds, etc.).

## How specifically does a fund work?

A fund – let's say it has $200 million, raised from 20 investors – would have a designated lifespan, usually 10 years. The fund (let's call it Tempus Fugit I) would invest in a number of companies (usually 20 to 30), making up a portfolio sufficient to spread out the risk for the investors.

The most common legal structure is a limited partnership in which the investors are limited partners (LPs), who provide almost all of the capital and have a passive role, and the VC firm is the general partner (GP) and has the responsibility of managing the fund. Usually GPs are required to provide some money for the fund. The most common investment breakdown of fund commitments is 1% from the GP and 99% from the LPs.

Most often the capital committed to the fund by the LPs will be called by the VC periodically to fund investments and expenses. By using this capital-call structure (versus calling all the money on day one), the internal rate of return to investors is improved. Usually the fund will have a specified final closing date on which the partners in the fund are finalized. While no more investors can be added after the final closing date, an LP can sell their investment along the way.

The fund will likely have an investment period in which the VC can call capital for new investments (normally three or four years). After this time, no new investments can be made, but follow-on investments in support of existing portfolio companies are okay. Once the VC has called all the capital (total commitments to Fund I), no additional capital may be requested from the investors in Fund I.

By the time the investment period for Fund I expires, the VC firm would have attempted to raise Fund II and possibly be thinking about Fund III. The limited partners in Fund I are under no obligation to invest in Tempus Fugit II.

Most venture funds contain a prohibition against cross-fund investing, meaning that if Fund I invested in your company, Fund II can't invest without special permission from the LPs.

In return for managing the fund, the general partner (the VC firm) will be paid an annual management fee, typically 2%–3% of committed capital. In addition, the GP receives an incentive fee (known as carried interest) calculated as a percentage of the profits on the fund. Twenty percent is the most common, but some top firms earn up to 30% of profits. There are many nuances to how profit is calculated and shared that are beyond the scope of this book.

## How is the money from a fund invested?

The money is invested over a period of several years in a number of companies, in stages. Using the example of Tempus Fugit I, which raised $200 million, the plan was to invest approximately 25% per year of the available funds over the course of four years.

Usually funds will allocate their anticipated investment in a company over several years, keeping money in reserve for subsequent investment rounds (referred to as "dry powder"). Although there is normally no legal (contractual) requirement that a venture fund invest in subsequent rounds of funding, there is often an expectation of participation.

Some funds have a strategy of only investing at a certain stage (e.g., seed only) and make it clear they will not participate in future rounds. As an entrepreneur, you have a right to – and you should – ask every investor how much capital they are reserving from their fund for investment in your company's future rounds.

## What does the fund get for its investment in a startup?

In return for its investment capital, the venture fund will receive an ownership stake, or shares (otherwise known as equity) in the startup. If the VC is leading the round and has the qualifications, that firm may also get a seat on the board. The limited partners are passive investors, with no oversight responsibility or opportunity. As the founder/CEO of a portfolio company of a venture firm, it is possible that you may never meet your VC's investors.

## What do founders get?

In addition to getting capital to develop their idea and grow the company, founders get advice, oversight, and perhaps additional resources from the VC firm. And, of course, founders keep equity in the company – a smaller piece of a bigger pie.

## When do LPs get returns from VC fund investments?

Limited partners get distributions from VC funds as portfolio companies of the fund achieve liquidity (go public in an IPO or are sold to a bigger company). The nature of venture capital is the expectation that some of the individual investments made from Tempus Fugit I would yield no return while a few others would generate very significant returns (see "power law" distribution, below).

## When does the VC firm/general partner get paid out?

In many funds, the general partner agrees to return all of the investors' capital before sharing in the upside. So, out of the $200 million Tempus Fugit I Fund, the general partner would have to return all $200 million to investors before seeing any carried interest. Some top VC firms with solid LP relationships (as a result of many years of strong investment performance) are permitted to take a percentage of profits on individual deals before all committed capital has been returned to LPs.

## When do founders see money?

The founders will see actual money when they sell their stake – their equity – in a company in an exit. Active founders (those who are working at the company in the interim) will also draw a salary.

As the length of time to exit a startup has increased, it has become common for investors to allow (and even encourage) founders and early management to sell some of their shares before the exit. Investors believe that taking the financial pressure off a founder who has worked for a decade (for low wages) building a startup will remove any impetus for the founder to seek an exit prematurely. As a result, a large market has developed for trading shares of privately held, venture-backed startups.

## Why do investors take such risks with venture capital?

Because the potential rewards are great. VCs are looking for home runs – not doubles or singles – with the expectation that many times they will strike out. In the world of statistics, this is known as a "power law" distribution, where almost all the returns are concentrated in a few deals. It's not a normal, bell-shaped curve.

LPs expect annual returns of around 15%–25% – some 5–15 percentage points above the returns they would have gotten from investing in a broad-based public stock market index over the same timeframe.

For the VCs, the return is not only financial. The earlier a VC firm invests in a company and the more active a role they play (e.g., holding a board seat), the more recognition they get as participating in the building of the company versus merely helping it to grow by investing.

\*\*\*

It might appear, based on the information presented in this chapter, that there is no downside to taking venture capital money. The investors assumed the bulk of the financial risk, while the founders invested their time, energy, and intellectual capital – which are significant investments in their own right.

That lack of financial risk for founders is one way of looking at it. But another way of thinking about it is that founders are not "giving" up equity; in a sense they are "selling" it, because every investor dilutes the percentage of their equity ownership stake. That's why some founders will choose taking on debt over taking VC money.

Also, there are entrepreneurs who not only want to keep the whole stake, but don't want a VC to tell them what to do at every monthly board meeting. There is a certain amount of control that an entrepreneur surrenders when they take venture capital.

Without doubt, the venture capital model has its downsides, for both founders and investors. That said, it has proven to be the best way to fuel and fund innovation, and it is why I believe venture capital combined with venture debt will continue to support the innovation ecosystem and America's economic engine.

## Key Takeaways

- Venture capitalists are looking for home runs in exchange for assuming financial risk.
- Founders need to be conscious of the implication of VCs taking equity stakes.
- Ask a VC if they will be reserving money for additional investment in your company.

# Chapter 9

## *Debt* Is Not a Four-Letter Word

As someone who has been working in growth/venture debt for more than 12 years, I can say that there are three major issues that frustrate me: venture debt isn't widely known, understood, or sufficiently used; it doesn't get its due as a critical part of the financial infrastructure; and it doesn't have the reputation it deserves. At best, it's seen as a commodity. At worst, it's seen as a bludgeon, wielded by predatory lenders.

"The industry has come very far in terms of education around funding," says Pixlee's Kyle Wong. "But when it comes to the details of funding versus the strategy of funding, I think there are still some missing pieces there."

Wong makes a key point regarding strategy, particularly around debt. When venture debt is used appropriately, it's an instrument that helps companies avoid dilution, and extend their runway. I really hope that after reading this book founders have a better understanding of the basics of financing overall, but also have a decent level of knowledge about venture debt.

Venture debt hasn't been in use as long as venture capital has. The latter dates back to the mid-1940s, while venture debt goes back to the 1970s. (If you're interested in the history of either, there are plenty of books about venture capital; and regarding venture debt, there are some in-depth resources online.)

I sometimes refer to venture debt as "growth debt" because it more clearly indicates what the money is for; "venture" sometimes evokes the idea of speculation, which to some extent is accurate, especially with regard to venture capital. But of course neither "venture" nor "growth" is the word that trips people up.

It's "debt." It's a word that usually has negative connotations. "To some extent, the idea that 'debt is bad' can be about an individual entrepreneur's values, how they were raised, or their fear that they'll screw up and not be able to service their debt," says Kelly Anderson, CEO of CXO Ventures. "It's funny because CEOs can get all hung up on valuation without realizing that debt can help boost valuation."

She also addresses one of the big arguments for debt: managing dilution. "So they're looking at valuation and running the numbers without thinking about how much equity they're giving up along the way."

Says Paul Schaut, a former serial CEO and now a professional board member, "I guide people toward it because it's a nondilutive form of funding that typically has some flexibility in it." That flexibility means you can use what you need, whereas with a traditional equity round, you could end up taking more money than you need, meaning more dilution than was warranted. In his experience, younger people are more aware of debt, but that doesn't necessarily mean that they fully understand it.

Paul rightly says that debt shouldn't be taken if a company doesn't feel confident in its ability to pay it back, doesn't understand the implications of debt, or is too far ahead of its target market. "Have you found repeatability and predictability in your business model, and therefore a revenue stream and cash flow?" He would counsel that a company not use debt without those pillars in place. "If you are too early and you haven't transitioned to that phase of your business, you will get caught up because debt comes with strings and covenants."

Frustrating as it is that founders often aren't aware of debt and its possibilities, it's not all that surprising. As one member of my team pointed out, many engineers (who more often than not are the founders of startups) don't understand capitalization, especially if they are a first-time founder. And venture debt represents a small fraction of the capitalization market.

However, it's not just first-time founders or relative novices who either don't know about debt or are new to it. Dan Doles, CEO of Mojix, who has been in Silicon Valley for more than 30 years and has been a CEO and/or founder of several other companies, used venture debt for the first time at Mojix, his most recent company.

"I had read about it, I had known about it, but I'd never done a venture debt deal," he says. "Traditionally, venture-backed technology companies would go to people like Silicon Valley Bank and get a line of credit against their AR [accounts receivable], or if you had physical assets like equipment and inventory, sometimes you could get a line of credit secured by those. But as long as you can be assured that you're going to be able to pay it back and service the debt at some point, venture debt is much more advantageous to the entrepreneur and founders than other forms."

Kelly says two deterrents to companies using venture debt are risk and a lack of understanding of how it differs from something like an SBA loan. "It comes down to whether the CEO is confident in their business plan and ability to execute to be able to make debt payments," she says. "Because if you're confident in your ability to pay, you should be doing debt all day long."

## Not Like Other Debt

Knowing how venture debt differs from other types of debt is key to understanding its utility. "For a lot of entrepreneurs at an earlier stage, they'll go through the SBA, where you're putting your house up for collateral," she says. "Whereas if you can understand more about venture debt and realize you're not doing those personal guarantees, that's a whole different ballgame than going the SBA route."

There are other ways in which venture debt differs from more familiar types of debt, such as a mortgage or a credit card. With either of those, the terms are going to be pretty similar regardless of which lender you go with. You might get a slightly better rate with one bank, or lower closing costs; with credit cards, the perks and annual fees may vary. But at their core, they're really not all that different.

That's not the case with venture debt lenders. And I would advise you to look beyond the rate. You want a lender who is going to take the time to get to know you and your business so together you can structure a deal that will benefit all parties. The structure of the loan is really important because if you default on your debt, you could lose your business. That's why you want to partner with a lender who has a reputation for being willing to work with you – which is not the case with all lenders.

---

## Different "Flavors" of Debt

According to Brandon Child, a managing director at Costella Kirsch, there are "different flavors of venture debt." Just as Runway lends to late- and growth-stage companies, Costella Kirsch lends to early-stage companies, mostly post-revenue.

Check sizes range from $500,000 to $5 million. "We will fund bootstrapped, angel-backed, or venture-backed companies," Brandon says. "We don't require there to be a fresh equity investment for us to write a venture debt check. Sometimes our loans are the first institutional capital that a company has ever received."

That's a differentiator to his firm; some venture debt lenders will only fund alongside a fresh equity raise.

While we at Runway lend to later-stage companies than Costella Kirsch does, like us, they are not in the "loan-to-own" business. "We really try to become partners in the business," says Brandon.

He describes the company as "fairly selective" regarding who they offer deals to, with an acceptance rate of 15%–20%. "It depends on the company and what their alternatives are," he says. "They may decide they want to raise equity, the board may decide they don't want debt, and if they've already taken venture money, the investors may want to put more money in."

Brandon notes that when a company has equity investors, the board has the final say in how the company capitalizes itself. "If they have strong conviction that the company is going to do extremely well, why wouldn't they want to put more of their dollars at work instead of having another company step in?" he asks rhetorically. "They get to buy more of the company because really what the founders are doing at that point is selling equity."

---

Jack Harding, after more than 20 years in Silicon Valley, speaks with some historical knowledge on the seamier side of venture debt lending and why it doesn't have a better reputation. "Venture debt overall has a bad reputation because there are too many companies out there who do 'loan to own,' loaning you money with very, very stringent terms and conditions, and the first time you stub your toe, they consider you in default and take the company," he says. "They sell off the assets and they liquidate it, and they might hire a trustee and milk some product lines for five years."

I'm not going to speak for other lenders. But owning your company is not our model, goal, or desire at Runway. Our goal with venture debt is to help companies grow. We like to think this is one of the distinctions of our brand. We operate with what we call an "equity mindset." I come out of the venture equity world and understand the ebb and flow of startups, the importance of patience and not panicking, and the need to collaborate to get past bumps in the road. And because venture-debt lenders aren't regulated (like banks), we have more freedom in how we structure and evaluate a deal.

Offers Jack, "I think there's an opportunity for the venture-debt folks to offer more education and evangelization [about] what they do because there's great value in providing nondilutive capital." He notes that when companies need to or should be exploring debt, it can be under a tight timeline or in a precarious situation. The more they know in advance, the better they can deal with what can be a very high-pressure, high-stakes set of circumstances.

Point taken, Jack.

Venture debt will never be as widely used as venture capital nor will it have the same immediate impact, but it should be used more often. It's not a case of one or the other, but both. Without venture capital, venture debt wouldn't exist. And without venture debt, lots of companies wouldn't make it to the finish line, meaning that the investors wouldn't recoup anything from their investment; owners' shares and those of other early shareholders (most likely early employees, and perhaps later employees with critical areas of expertise) would be heavily, heavily diluted – or wiped out entirely.

Venture debt makes it possible for companies to grow, creating more wealth to circulate through the economy. I am a businessman, and I am interested in supporting entrepreneurs and making money for my investors and my team. I feel good about that; and as a company we pride ourselves on doing so fairly, ethically, and responsibly.

In the hope that venture debt will be better known, understood, and more widely used, we at Runway will do our best to help companies grow and educate people throughout the ecosystem, allowing them to make good decisions, and create scenarios where everyone can win.

## Key Takeaways

- Venture debt is not widely enough known, understood, or used.
- The idea of "debt" can frighten away companies that could benefit from using venture debt judiciously.
- If not paid back, venture debt can put a company's assets at risk, but not an owner's personal assets.

# Chapter 10

# What a Deal with Debt Looks Like

For all the mystery around venture debt, doing a deal is usually a relatively straightforward process. In this chapter, I will demystify it further. The first thing to know about venture debt lenders is that the world is divided into early-stage lenders and late-stage lenders.

My business, Runway Growth Capital, lends to late-stage and growth-stage companies because our investors appreciate the added protection (lower risk) associated with larger, more mature companies. While the average company we lend to is 13 years old and has revenues averaging in excess of $50 million, they have yet to reach profitability.

Although they are still investing in growth, there's a path to profitability and sufficient evidence around both the technology underpinning the company and the business model to be able to make an informed decision.

While Runway is focused on the most mature pre-profit companies, other venture lenders focus on earlier-stage companies. For example, Brandon Child, with Costella Kirsch, targets very-early-stage businesses with strong prospects for future growth. He says there is a common perception among bootstrapped and angel-backed companies that you can get venture debt only if you've raised capital. "While that's often the case, it's not always true," he says. "If a non-venture-backed company comes to us, we're going to look at the company, not the capitalization table."

Specifically, as part of their analysis, they'll look for meaning-ful customer engagement, growth, modest cash burn, and low or no existing debt. "As long as those things seem like they're a fit, then we'll go into further diligence."

## Getting Started

Deal-making is very often about who you know – which also trans-lates into who knows you. This is especially true in the startup world and, fairly or not, the ecosystem that I wrote about in Chapter 5 can seem like a closed club. The most common way for us to get a debt deal is for a VC to contact us and say, "Hey, one of my companies or one of my partners' companies is raising debt. You guys should talk." For us, that's a good enough recommenda-tion for us to start the process.

The second most common way we get started with a deal is that we'll get contacted by a middleman – such as a boutique investment bank or a lawyer – acting on behalf of a company seek-ing debt. There are probably a handful of law firms – and maybe 20 lawyers among them – who do 80% of the legal documentation of venture-debt deals, so they are in a good position to advise a company seeking debt.

> The small number of lawyers and law firms who specialize in venture-debt deals will be a good source of information about lenders. Even if your potential lender isn't using a lawyer, I would still recommend that you ask your lawyer about the lender.

We also get deals from venture-debt-placement firms. They're part of a new class of financial-services firms that do nothing but help place debt for venture-backed companies. Such firms are a subset of the boutique investment banks mentioned above.

## Why Using a Third Party Can Make Sense

Even experienced VCs aren't always very knowledgeable about debt, which is why it can make sense to use a third party to guide and advise you through the process. One such company with whom I've worked in my capacity as a VC is Armentum Partners. The Menlo Park–based company structures debt financing and raises debt capital for emerging technology and biotech growth companies.

"Most of the businesses that we work with have raised some sort of venture capital, usually multiple rounds," says Hutch Corbett, a managing partner at Armentum. "We help companies access the debt market, educating them about various sources of debt and introducing them to the best lenders for their specific needs."

The debt that Armentum raises – on which the borrower pays them a fee – could be from a bank or a nonbank fund like Runway. "Typically, the product that we raise is a complement to equity, not a replacement," says Hutch. "I call it enterprise value debt because it's cash-flow-dependent." He points out that biotech companies can get debt financing pre-revenue, but on the technology side – such as with an SaaS offering – being able to access debt depends on having product-market fit and being able to scale revenue.

Why should a business spend more for its money by using a third party such as Armentum? That's a fair question – and one I asked Hutch when I first worked with him. In addition to knowing various groups of lenders in both the traditional capital markets and the alternative markets (which Runway is part of), their focus on raising debt means they often have strong relationships with both lenders and VCs.

"Lenders like to work with us because if we get hired, it shows the board is serious about raising capital and everyone knows a deal is going to happen," says Hutch. "It's going to be a competitive process where we can offer guidance and support, as the best alternative may not be readily apparent."

According to Hutch, there has been a change in how much he ends up explaining debt as an option versus which debt option would be best for a company. "It's not like a light switch has gone on and off, but it's been more of a gradual shift," he says. "The momentum is growing with new providers coming into the market."

That may mean more competition for Runway, but in my opinion, it's still a plus for everyone.

Again – and I will stress this over and over – at any stage where you are going outside your "friends and family" circle for money, you want to work with people who are well-connected and experienced. They will have access to other people who can help you, and the better known they are, the easier it is to check them out in terms of reputation and trustworthiness.

## The Process

The first step in the process of raising venture debt is a quick, introductory filtering phone call between you and the potential lender that's an equal amount selling and listening – on both sides. Think of it like a first date. Should that go well, it should then be followed up quickly with both parties signing an NDA. (VCs don't like to sign NDAs but venture debt lenders don't have a problem with it.)

At this point, we would start our initial due diligence. We typically ask a company for six things:

1. **An investor presentation**

   If you are looking for investment money, you probably have recently raised equity. The investor deck you would have used for that works for venture debt as well. (There are numerous examples online.)

2. **The 409A**

   The annual valuation of the equity value of the company, designed to protect employees who are granted stock options so that they can't later be slapped with a tax for getting "cheap stock." Usually those valuations come in at a level that makes getting equity attractive to employees. Don't worry if the value assigned by the 409A valuation firm is lower than what you believe is fair. We know how these valuations work and don't become fixated on their valuation.

   The 409A will include different ways of analyzing the value of the company, the same things we look at: discounted future cash flow; comparables to public companies; comparables to recent M&A. It will also give a really good history of all the funding the company's ever gotten, and it always includes a five-year projection.

3. **A detailed capitalization table and funding history**

   This will include everybody who owns any piece of the company, a history of fundraising, and a history of any bank financing or external debt used.

4. **Historical financials**

Ideally, we will receive five years of historical financial statements. We would love it if they were audited, but it's not necessary.

5. **Projected financials**

For us to do our work, we want a fully linked, three-statement financial model. The three statements are: balance sheet, income statement, and statement of cash flow. If there are delays or issues in the process, it's usually because of a delay in getting linked three-statement projections, which allows us to do "what-if" analyses (such as: "If things go worse than planned, when do things break? How much does this startup need to reduce their variable expenses to remain viable and able to service our debt?").

Often we're lending to companies that sell to big enterprises, so instead of having a million customers they've got a hundred, and we'll want to understand how they sell, how predictable their sales forecasts are, and how comfortable they are with the coming years. All of that helps us judge how much we believe in their financial projections.

6. **A list of the largest customers, present and past**

Detailed customer information allows us to identify customer concentration or churn. Those can be quick disqualifiers, and we don't want to waste a lot of anyone's time if that's the case.

If a potential borrower's customer base is too concentrated (fewer than 15 total customers or more than 50% of revenues from just a few customers), that's too risky for us. Or if the startup has a lot of churn – meaning that their existing customers decided they're not going to renew or stay with them – that's another red flag/likely disqualifier. There is nuance around this, too. If your product has evolved significantly and in what we would consider a positive, logical direction, then churn could make sense.

With all this information, we can do a desktop analysis that typically takes two weeks. We could do it more quickly if absolutely necessary, but we like to give ourselves two weeks. If the desktop analysis is positive, we would issue a term sheet.

Doing it our way allows us to customize a thoughtful structure and set of terms that are fair for us and appropriate for the borrower. For example, tailoring the loan for the borrower could be around when you actually need the money. Maybe you need it right away, or perhaps it's a little further down the road. Other variations could mean structuring the deal so the interest rate declines as the company gets stronger, or having a longer interest-only period, where the debt isn't amortizing, because you wouldn't be in a position to start to amortize until a certain event occurs.

I would estimate that everything I've outlined above should take about four to five weeks from our first phone call. That means you'd probably have a term sheet by Week 5.

## Going to the Board

Up until now you'd probably only have the CEO and CFO involved. Once you get a term sheet, you'd want to present the deal to the board.

Some companies will have their board involved from the beginning of the process. I've known of deals that got derailed because a board member didn't want to do a deal with a specific lender. It could be a personal (and one-sided) beef; it could be that a board member knows something specific about the lender. This has never happened to us, which is why I suggest at least letting your board know what lenders you're talking to early in the process.

How quickly things move from the board presentation step depends on the borrower. They'll likely be looking over term sheets from different lenders. I would guess 10% of the time we're the only lender involved. The other 90% of the time there are multiple lenders pitching to provide growth capital. The company may also be considering using some or all equity to meet their needs.

If there are three or four term sheets to work through and compare, you will probably take about a week to get through those. While a deal itself may be relatively straightforward, that doesn't mean that every deal will be the same. Not only do lenders differ regarding the stage at which they will lend money, but some will also specialize by industry. Terms will, of course, vary from lender to lender.

For example, if you are looking at a lender, a key question to ask is, "What is your ratio of term sheets to closed deals?" This should give you a sense of how seriously you should take any overture. (A sample term sheet – a mostly nonbinding agreement outlining the basic terms and conditions surrounding a potential investment – that we would use is in the Appendix.) There are lenders who will offer term sheets just to get their foot in the door. We don't do term sheets unless we're pretty confident that we're going to do the deal. For example, in 2022 we signed 15 term sheets and closed all but two. One remains in process as of publication and the other decided not to use debt because their board wasn't confident in the company's ability to predict its business and achieve its plan.

---

Some lenders blow hot and cold or will issue term sheets that don't really amount to anything. The issuing of a term sheet doesn't come with legal obligations on the lender's part, but we like companies to know that if we've gone to the trouble of doing the work required for a term sheet to be issued, chances are really high that we want to do business with them.

This has worked to our advantage in building our reputation as being a steady hand in choppy waters, and about being more than merely transactional. VCs and board members are looking for money (and partners) they can count on.

---

There are only two aspects of the term sheet that are binding, as term sheets are pretty standard throughout the business. The first is a period of exclusivity – say 30 days – where it says that the potential borrower won't work with any other lender while we do our due diligence.

The other binding part is that the potential borrower is required to make a deposit with us, usually ranging from $50,000 to $100,000. Our guarantee is that if *we* walk away in due diligence, we'll refund all of the money except for what we spent on due diligence. Such expenses are usually minimal. If the borrower pulls out, they forfeit their deposit.

That puts it at Week 6 for a signed term sheet. All that's left from there is what we call "confirmatory due diligence" and legal documentation. The variability in the legal documents versus the variability in term sheets is very minimal. (Almost all of the legal documentation around term sheets can be traced back to the work of one lawyer, John Hale. Most people probably haven't heard of him, but his work has had a big impact on deal-making in Silicon Valley.)

The number of negotiating items is relatively small, so getting through that part should be fairly quick. If you are planning to use venture debt, you will want to make sure you're using an attorney with experience negotiating venture debt loan agreements. They aren't very complex, but they are very specific, and much time and money can be wasted if one side of the table is being educated on the job.

As part of the final due diligence, most lenders will do an on-site visit. At Runway, it's mandatory that we spend one to two days at the company and meet the entire senior management team. In my mind, looking the team (especially the CEO, CFO, and head of sales) in the eye and going through their customer base line-by-line is critical. I'm proud to say that we maintained this process throughout the pandemic.

As the final phase of due diligence, the last thing we do is reference checks with the company's customers. We'll call maybe 10 to 15 customers to confirm what the company has told us. If we can, we'll do reference checks with customers that the company has lost. This isn't about playing gotcha. We just want to do everything we can to try to get a feel for the company's reputation in the marketplace. If the company is nonsponsored – meaning they haven't raised any institutional money – we'll do a full background check on management as well.

These last two stages – after Week 6 – can take another four to six weeks. And then, if all goes well, we'll close, and the borrower will have the money wired to their account on the day of closing. In total, expect the process to last from 10 to 12 weeks from the first meeting to cash in the bank.

## How Much?

At Runway, we're enterprise value lenders – enterprise value being how much the company is worth. We'll lend a company up to 25% of its value. From our perspective, the durability of enterprise value is more important than the potential for a big upside.

It's also important to know that we tend to ignore (or at least underweight) the value of the company defined in the most recent round of equity funding, especially if the round was priced by existing or strategic investors or was more than a year earlier. For us, the most important definer of value is relevant and recent M&A comps. We will also look at public comps, DCF (discounted cash flow) analysis, sum-of-the-parts, and other mechanisms of ascribing value, but the most important is M&A comps (because the most likely means of exit for venture-backed companies is M&A).

## The Interest-Only Period

Almost all venture-debt deals come with an interest-only (IO) period. It is an important structural element of a growth loan because it provides the borrower with more cash to use to fund growth (compared to if the loan required amortization – principal payments – from day one). As you can imagine, most borrowers prefer as long an IO period as possible. It provides the most flexibility and the most access to capital. To accommodate this desire, most of our deals include provisions for automatic extension of the IO period if the loan and borrower are performing as planned. From our perspective, if we have a borrower we like, we're going to work to keep them, which usually means extending the interest-only period.

Unfortunately for borrowers, many lenders have a very different philosophy – "We get in and we get out" – and view the velocity of debt as a good thing. They generally couch it by saying something like "Technology changes so fast. It's just our way of managing risk."

To me, that's an excuse. It's one thing if a borrower's risk profile changes dramatically, but very often that's not the case. Beware of lenders with a reputation for being rigid about amortization. It is probably an indication that they expect that you will refinance them at the end of the IO period.

## Covenants Are Your Friend

Borrowers could save themselves a lot of pain if they worked with their lenders to develop properly structured covenants. Too often borrowers view themselves as having scored a big win if they have no covenants: "We got a deal at prime plus one with no covenants."

Covenants – agreements between two parties about what each will and will not do – protect both borrowers and lenders. Be very wary of a lender who doesn't have covenants. They pretty much say, "Here's the money. We don't care what you do with it, but if things go wrong, remember, we're first money out."

Communication protocols are another way of making the relationship a strong, positive one for both parties, which is why we build them into our covenants. We normally have a performance covenant that is designed to lead to a discussion if you are not achieving a specified percentage (typically 85%) of a mutually agreed upon financial plan.

If you have a loan with Runway or any other lender, at the end of every month your CFO will be required to file a compliance certificate, stating that there are no defaults, no fraud, and how the company is doing relative to its goals. Let's say at the end of August we get the certificate for July, and it essentially says, "We're in default" (compliance certificates are typically due 30 days after the end of the month). Our normal response would be to set up a call with the CEO and CFO to find out what's going on. We might hear something like, "Oh, a couple of big accounts slipped from July. Wait until you get the August certificate, and you'll see that we'll be back on plan." Very often, the slip fixes itself and we waive the default and move on.

However, if at the end of September, we were to get the August certificate and it was the same story, we would have another conversation – this one a little more serious. We might have a conversion with the company and include the VC sponsors. We might suggest that we recalibrate everyone's expectations and establish a new official plan for the company. We might also ask the VCs to invest some additional capital to maintain the liquidity profile (runway) on which we based our underwriting.

When companies have missed projections for two months, putting the quarter in jeopardy, it's not uncommon for the CEO to declare "all hands on deck" to make sure that September results are spectacular. There's every chance that September won't be spectacular. In that case, we might have a conversation about making some amendments to the loan and/or hiring a banker to sell the company.

Selling the company prematurely is nobody's desired outcome, so the communication protocols (defined in the covenants) would ensure that there will be no surprises after the first missed month. Without such protocols and covenants, it's too easy for things to slip under the rug – often without malicious intent, and with the sincere belief that things will pick up. The lender might realize too late that the borrower has missed their revenue for six months and is now in dire straits.

Those kinds of circumstances usually mean there is not enough time to sell the company in an orderly process that maximizes value for all constituents. Too often in this situation, lenders, in shock from the revelation that a borrower they thought was doing fine was actually in crisis, will panic, foreclose on the company, and attempt to sell the assets in a fire sale, which isn't good for anyone's reputation.

At Runway, we have built our reputation on not panicking. Instead, we pride ourselves on being a steady hand in rough seas and doing everything possible to be patient and a good partner. We may not always agree, but we will always listen and work tirelessly to find a mutually workable solution.

## Key Takeaways

- Borrowing is a fairly straightforward process, but each lender may offer different terms.
- It is wise to involve your board from the beginning of your process to consider debt.
- Covenants and communication protocols will protect both parties.

# Chapter 11

## Making the Most of Debt

There are three maxims that everyone should understand when it comes to taking on debt:

No. 1: You should raise debt when you *can* raise equity, but you choose not to.

No. 2: Don't pursue debt because you can't raise equity.

No. 3: Debt is a double-edged sword.

Says Rob Winkelmann, managing partner and CEO of debt-consulting firm Credo 180°, "Debt can be really helpful to companies, but it can also be detrimental." He says that his team doesn't persuade companies one way or the other when it comes to debt. "We do analysis," he says. "To us, it's a math question."

Notes Armentum's Hutch Corbett, "As the market has evolved, debt has become a much more strategic financing tool, in part because of the amounts of money that companies can borrow and the longer-term flexibility that allows it to be part of the capital structure."

Venture debt in particular is a powerful instrument when you take it at the right time, for the right reason, and when the lender is the right one for you. Under those circumstances, you'll have the opportunity to make the most of debt: extend your runway, avoid additional dilution, help your company grow until it's time to make an exit (or a better time to raise equity). This chapter is to help you understand how to make the most of debt.

Just as equity isn't always the best answer, debt isn't, either. "You see a lot of younger entrepreneurs pursuing a venture debt product when they really shouldn't," says Paul Schaut. "If they don't have sufficient repeatability or predictability levels, the company is not ready to take on the governance levels associated with debt."

Second, make sure you take debt from the right lender, and the right kind of lender. Just as all money is not created equal, all lenders are not created equal. Any lender has an enormous amount of control and power. If you're in default, the lender might have the ability to take over your bank accounts and even sweep all the cash.

The good news is that there are steps you can take that will go a long way toward ensuring that taking debt is a positive for your company. These include better educating yourself about debt overall, finding out about the reputation of lenders and their specific business models, and seeking advice from your investors. "My job is to educate and inform boards and provide facts," says Credo 180°'s Rob Winkelmann. "It's to share what knowledge we have about various lenders and never use competitive banter, or market banter, but specific, fact-based situations known to us in terms of how lenders have behaved or not."

For example, Rob will know how a certain lender behaved in a situation where a company couldn't service its debt. In some cases, such situations may end up being redeemable, depending on the relationships with your lenders, and your and your lenders' appetite for risk. I'll go through some scenarios for how such situations can be redeemed.

## Extending Your Runway

For Kamakshi Sivaramakrishnan, co-founder of Drawbridge, which helps businesses identify when an individual is using multiple devices, venture debt only became a possibility after the company had raised a seed round of $1 million, topped it off with a Series A of $6.5 million, and was going into Series B. "By then we had become a revenue-generating company, hitting about $30–$40 million of revenue," she remembers. "The concept of collateralized debt was introduced to me, and along the way came the notion of venture debt."

Like Mojix, Drawbridge took venture debt during a time of transition. "We had converted our business model from a hybrid product/service business model to an SaaS model," Kamakshi says. "We converted from the two-prong business model to a singular business model by divesting our product business and shutting down product support."

She recalls that in shutting down product support, the company initially lost about 90% of its revenue. "It was actually a low-margin business and to really grow, we needed to invest only in the SaaS model," she says.

Such a transition is challenging for any business, Kamakshi acknowledges, but she and her team had a high degree of confidence that making the switch to SaaS only would pay off.

"Confident as we were, we needed about a year's time to really make it work," she says. "Venture debt worked out to be a great option for us in this circumstance because VC folks would have devalued the company tremendously in that 'transition/proof' period because our revenues were so heavily – but temporarily – reduced."

She describes venture debt as "expensive, but not costly," given the company's circumstances. "It turned out to be a win all-around. It gave us the time we needed to prove our new business model, which proved to be so attractive that we got acquired by LinkedIn at a valuation we never would have received when we needed the money."

Runway got paid back, the VCs made money on their investment, and by avoiding both dilution and devaluation, the employees' stakes in the company ended up being worth more.

## Be Realistic

Things typically go wrong with borrowing as a result of a startup being overly optimistic about their forecast. This can be partially driven by not taking the time to make what we call a bank plan – a more realistic plan than what you'd give to a VC.

It's not uncommon for a company to have a five-year projection that's used as the basis for venture investment. Usually it's overly optimistic because the VC model is about growth first, and profits later. When we see an overly optimistic plan, we'll tell the founders, "We're going to set covenants against these numbers. If you're not going to meet these expectations, why not tell us that now?"

But most of the time they can't resist. I would guess 90% of companies initially fail to meet the plans they give us, so it's not something we're surprised by. Companies are more concerned about not disappointing venture investors, who after all are their owners, bosses, and board members, than they are about disappointing us.

## Be Confident

You shouldn't borrow money unless you have confidence in your business. If deep down you are more hopeful than confident, stick with venture capital. Even if you're confident about the business model and the technology but you're not confident about timing, equity is a better option.

Let's say you're developing the next generation of your product. You know there's a market for it, and maybe your customers are already asking for it and are committed to it. You also know that your development team has never been good at meeting deadlines. That's an example of being confident in demand for the technology but not the timing. Equity is driven by hope in a way that debt isn't and is also more patient. When timing is uncertain, you need capital that is going to be patient.

You might be tempted to take a loan when there's no more venture capital available to you. Your lead VC might have become disenchanted with your business and is unwilling to invest any further, or they could come back to you and say, "Yes, we love you, but we don't have any more money, so you need to find another VC to lead the next round." Either way you need a new source of funds and raising another round of venture capital can be a lengthy, difficult process.

Every day we see companies interested in debt because they think it will be quicker and easier than seeking additional equity investment. Taking on debt for the sake of expediency rather than to avoid dilution can be dangerous because you probably won't take the time to research lenders properly and/or take the time to negotiate and structure an optimal deal.

In a perfect world, your VCs, especially your board members, will steer you away from taking debt at the wrong time, or from a lender who isn't right for you. But there are investors who, despite their experience and sophistication in other aspects of financing, don't give you optimal advice about debt.

That's why it's up to you to educate yourself and remember what debt can do for you, especially when it comes to minimizing dilution, and what it can't do for you. "The idea of debt is to give companies access to more cash, which means a longer cash runway before they have to raise more money," says Rob Winkelmann. "That in turn means they either hit more milestones if things go well, or if things take longer, or there's some problems or hiccups, it allows them to get through those things, and still hit that inflection point before they have to raise their next round."

Debt, Rob notes, can't compensate for certain facts: for example, if you haven't hit certain milestones or are already too debt-heavy. Nor can it magically make raising your next round of equity easier. "If you've got a lot of debt, new investors are going to want to know right away who is going to take care of that existing debt."

## Timing Is Everything

During his time working at Sir Kensington, a condiment company that he helped start, Brandon Child (now a managing director at Costella Kirsch) and his partners raised capital numerous times, never using venture debt. "We didn't really know it was an option," says Brandon. "We were often getting valued on trailing 12 months' revenue. And our business, which was really centered on barbecuing, was somewhat seasonal." As the founders were looking into using debt for the first time, Sir Kensington was acquired.

Because of the seasonality of the business in most parts of the country, meaning its sales were highest in summer, Sir Kensington often had to raise equity for working capital requirements in the spring. "We were selling a physical product that was seasonal, not software," acknowledges Brandon.

But giving up equity instead of raising debt had its consequences. "When you're getting valued on trailing 12 months' revenue and you have to raise money right before your busy season, you're leaving something on the table by selling equity at a discount," he says.

"If we had known about venture debt, we may have been able to use it to increase the value of our company at the times that we were raising equity by simply capitalizing the company slightly differently. That is one of the things that turned me on to the value of venture debt for certain companies, and also made me realize that the timing for when you choose to raise equity is very important."

## Know What Kind of Lender You're Dealing With

Part of using debt wisely is understanding the reputation and the model of any lender you're contemplating taking money from. As with any other step of the process, you need to do your own due diligence. On the lender side, there are plenty out there that just want to close loans. They're not thinking about whether taking on that debt is good for you.

"We did a lot of reference calls with different founders to understand what happens when things go poorly," says Pixlee's Kyle Wong. "But I think as a founder, you have a responsibility to understand venture debt is not the same as equity, and you shouldn't kind of spend it or think about it the same way."

There are lenders who are very upfront about their unwillingness to work with borrowers. One infamous story in Silicon Valley is about the lender who swept cash on Christmas Day – cash that had been personally injected into the borrowing company by one of the partners at a top-tier venture firm to allow the borrower to make payroll. The reputation of the lender was pretty much destroyed.

As with almost any industry, there is a range of participants, some more aggressive than others. In venture lending, the most aggressive players (those that take the most risk and ask for most in return) are sometimes described as "loan to own" lenders. They play an important role in that they are willing to take risks that Runway would never take. For example, ESW Capital, a consolidator of software businesses that also makes loans (with a view toward an acquisition), offers one-year loans at very favorable rates to SaaS companies. But they state, right up front, "If you don't pay us back in a year, we own your company."

Everyone involved knows the deal. It's hard money, but it might be the only option and might be the capital that makes the difference. Worst case, the borrower has a buyer lined up. There are other loan-to-own lenders, whose model is all about taking on greater risk than a more conservative lender would.

We at Runway put ourselves in the conservative category. At the same time, we pride ourselves on thinking like equity people when it comes to patience. Borrowers have come back to us and said, "We're not going to meet our plan. Our development team didn't get it done." When that happens, we'll dig in and try to understand why and probably reset our expectations.

We analyze the worst-case scenario – you can't pay back your debt – not with an eye toward owning. We're looking at it from the perspective of "If things don't work out, who are the most likely buyers? What will they pay? How fast could the company be sold? How quickly can a home for this company be found?"

## What to Watch For

Debt doesn't go wrong all at once. It's a progressive situation. If you start not meeting your plan, ideally, you're going to get a call from the lender saying, "Hey, we noticed:

- You've been missing your top-line number.
- You've been missing your bottom-line number.
- Your churn has been higher than normal.
- The whole engineering team is leaving.

Or, better yet, when you notice any of these things (or other signs), you proactively reach out to your lender and bring them into the conversation. Depending on how communicative and forthright you are, that conversation could be friendly, or tense. The advice that I'll offer – just as I have for many other circumstances – is to be open and honest. You will quickly become aware of the difference between bank and nonbank lenders in these situations.

If you're with a nonbank lender, you will usually be speaking with decision makers. At a bank, you might be immediately thrown into a workout group. Nonbank lenders, like Runway, are able to meet with your investors to find a solution to the default. Possible solutions could include them working with your lender to readjust the covenants, or a compromise where the lenders agree to give you more time, and the venture guys put in more money to support the extended timeframe. These are fairly common scenarios with nonbank lenders.

Sometimes companies in default look for another lender. We had a situation where somebody owed us $10 million, and it was clear their business wasn't going anywhere. They tried to sell the company, but nobody would buy it for the price that the VCs wanted. They found another lender to lend them $7 million, and the VCs put up the other $3 million to pay us off.

## Bank Money? Don't Bank on It

First, let me say that banks are an absolutely essential part of the financial infrastructure. They play a critical role that can't be filled by anyone else, and I'm not talking the basics like holding your accounts. They can lend money more inexpensively than non-bank lenders like Runway can.

On the other hand, banks are not nearly as flexible. "Depending on the state of the economy, it's either the business development side of the company that is in charge, or the credit side," says Paul Schaut. "You don't want to be tripping covenants when the credit side is in charge."

Banks have workout groups whose sole job is to work with companies when a loan goes bad. The person who you dealt with in originating your loan – your relationship manager – will be completely out of the picture and powerless, rendering the title "relationship manager" meaningless and ironic. The very clinical workout group will want to get repaid as quickly as possible.

Another potential downside to banks is they're regulated, not self-governed. If regulators pass down an edict that changes a bank's appetite for risk, you might be notified that your credit line has been pulled, regardless of how diligent you've been about servicing your debt. You'll be given a limited amount of time to pay back the money.

This scenario played out with internet companies (as they were called in 2000–2001) and in the clean-tech space in around 2011. Many VCs tell me that situations like this are why they won't work with banks anymore and prefer non-bank lenders.

There's room for all kinds of players in the lending space – provided they are honest and transparent. The model we've developed at Runway has worked not only for us, but for the businesses we've helped grow.

I didn't go into venture debt because it's a sure way to make money. I chose it because the way we practice it, it's a sure way to help companies grow. And when our borrowers do well, we do well.

## Key Takeaways

- Equity can be more patient than debt – but it costs more.
- Different lenders have different models and goals. Know your lender!
- Defaulting on your loan can leave you and your investors with nothing.

# Chapter 12

## Options for Exits

*Ley took a chance by not selling 19/39 when Unicorn came calling, but it was a calculated risk. He had always viewed a sale as his exit strategy, but the company was on a promising trajectory, so selling to Unicorn would be premature. He had experienced, knowledgeable board members advising him and backing him up in his plan to wait to sell. The company's first-mover status, early success, and popular product all worked to Ley's and the company's advantage and were reasons that the board advised him to hold out.*

*By the time 4Paws' CEO Nickerson decided to sell to Unicorn, his company didn't hold the same potential it once did. Nickerson had imagined that his company would one day go public; he had long dreamed of being the CEO of a publicly traded company. However, the reality of missed milestones, exhausted employees, and tired investors forced him to sell. Had Nickerson not sold to Unicorn, he would have had to find new investors, which would have further diluted his equity stake.*

\*\*\*

You should begin with the end in mind. Venture capitalists and growth lenders do. They have a vision for what an exit – a liquidity event – might look like and when it might occur. Founders should, too – right from the start. VC investors, especially seed and early-stage folks, may not want to talk about it or hear you talk about it, but rest assured, they are thoughtful about exit options. Early planning can help you structure your business toward the desired outcome.

After taking venture capital, your exit path will almost certainly be one of the following:

- M&A: A sale to another company. Consideration may be cash, shares in the acquiring company, or a combination. The buyer may be a public or private company.
- Initial public offering (IPO).
- Dissolution (wind down the company).

I guess it is theoretically possible that a startup could continue to operate indefinitely as an independent, private company. According to Crunchbase, 406 such companies (founded before 1990 and raised more than $20 million in venture equity) are active in the United States as of December 2022.

Having a solid exit plan also allows external investors – VCs, angels, friends and family – to make calculations around their own timeline and the hoped-for rate of return on their investment. This will make you more attractive to potential investors and lenders. Secondly, deciding how and at what point you want to exit enables you to optimize the return for all stakeholders. The exact timing of your exit is largely out of your control, but having a plan minimizes floundering and provides a compass when making key decisions on your long journey.

Of the potential scenarios mentioned here, the most likely outcome for a startup is failure. That's the harsh reality, but you already knew that. Venture-backed startups are less likely to fail than nonsponsored ones. Of successful exits of venture-backed startups, M&A is the most likely outcome. According to Crunchbase, of the 23,206 companies in the United States that raised more than $10 million of venture equity since 1990, 6,905 (30%) were acquired while 2,010 (8.7%) went public. The remainder failed or continue to operate as private companies. That said, the exit strategy founders usually focus on is the IPO. Most CEOs use the goal of an IPO to plant an aspirational flag around which to rally the troops toward achieving an aggressive, rewarding common goal.

Being IPO-ready and -worthy will make you a more valuable acquisition target. That's why it's smart to lead your business toward an IPO, even though an acquisition offer may appear just before or in the years following your IPO.

A big advantage to going public is the branding, publicity, and marketing associated with the process. Even if your company is relatively small, or not a household name, being able to say "We're a public company" catches the attention of potential clients, your peers, and the media, and gives you a certain amount of street cred.

Going public means an infusion of capital from new sources, as there is now literally a public market for shares in your company. Down the road, should you wish to raise additional capital, you can issue more shares – provided your share price reflects a healthy (and realistic) optimism about the future. Such additional capital can be used to pay off debt, finance an acquisition or other growth-related initiatives, or merely shore up your war chest for later use.

In more practical terms, being a public company means your company's value will be determined by its share price. The sky-high expectations around valuation and growth that often are part of the private investment phase now give way to (usually) more realistic projections around revenue and growth, as CEOs and boards of publicly traded companies are held to high standards of transparency regarding projections and performance. Instead of answering to your lead investors – and lenders, should you have chosen to take debt – you're now accountable to thousands of investors.

Finally, going public is a form of liquidity for early shareholders, although not an immediate one. All of these possibilities are predicated on the idea that your company and share price remain healthy.

## Cons

You're now accountable to thousands of investors. The company's actions and those of senior management will be under scrutiny from the public, research analysts, the SEC, and other regulatory bodies.

There's a saying that an IPO is an "illiquidity event" for insiders or management because you'll be locked up (prevented from selling your shares) for anywhere from six months to a year (although in some cases, it could be longer).

If your goal is to cash out and you're looking toward the IPO path, be prepared to do it over a long a period of time. Even after the IPO lock-up period expires, senior management ("insiders") will be restricted to selling only in very specific windows. The SEC assumes that in the last few weeks of a quarter insiders will know what the quarter looks like while outsiders don't, which is why there's a window preceding each quarterly earnings release when you'll be prohibited from selling.

After a short period, usually the second day after you announce your quarterly earnings and file your 10-Q for another 20 trading days, when the SEC considers all available information to be in the public domain (the "open window" period), insiders can buy or sell. The window will close again after 20 trading days.

There are numerous rules and regulations around insiders selling shares of publicly traded companies, and those that are in effect now may not be when your time comes to do so. Tax and compensation experts can help you in setting up and executing plans for insider sales. When insiders, especially founders, start selling big chunks of stock, it can send a negative signal to the market, so the process needs to be carefully managed.

Other cons to going public:

**The IPO may be priced wrong.** Bill Gurley, a well-known VC at Benchmark, has been a vocal, outspoken critic of the IPO process. He has asserted numerous times that the reason so many companies have such a big price bump immediately following an IPO is because the IPO is actually underpriced. He maintains that underwriters have an incentive to do this in order to give their best institutional clients a windfall.

**Everything for the management team becomes about "beat and raise."** When you give projections to the investment bankers during the IPO, those figures will be shared with the research team and are then incorporated in the financial projections that are shared with potential buyers as part of the IPO process and in future research reports. Following the IPO, your goal becomes about beating those targets and raising them every quarter.

There comes a point at which there is only so much land left to conquer; eventually, it becomes virtually impossible to achieve a certain level of growth in perpetuity. I've been told it's usually about 15 quarters for the very best companies before the math stops working. Another problem, discussed in the next few paragraphs, is that during this same time frame, you will likely transition from being valued in the market on a multiple of revenues to a multiple of earnings. If this doesn't go well, you might triple the size of the company in four or five years only to see your valuation remain flat from the IPO.

The most common metric for valuing publicly traded stocks is the price-to-earnings (PE) ratio, but because many venture-backed companies go public before they are profitable, the investment bankers will look to other metrics to establish the value for your IPO. Most often, you will be valued on a multiple of your revenues at the time of your IPO. Comparisons to similar, already-public companies will likely be the principal factor in determining your price-to-sales multiple.

Other metrics that will impact your value are rate of sales growth, gross margins, predictability of future revenues and earnings (when they come), and any competitive advantages you might have (such as patents, customer base, etc.).

All companies, whether public or private, are eventually valued on their ability to generate cash flow. After you go public and you fight the uphill battle against "beat and raise," you'll be fighting another battle as well: the transition from being valued mainly on price-to-sales to being valued on price-to-earnings.

When you start to get valued on a multiple of earnings, the math of making that transition is incredibly difficult, and frequently leads to a painful, frustrating, precipitous decline in your stock price. Accomplishing both "beat and raise" and transitioning from price-to-sales to price-to-earnings is very challenging. Welcome to the world of being a public company CEO/CFO.

**It's an unpleasant process.** That's an understatement. Beyond just the sheer number of hours required, there's just a lot of seemingly unnecessary BS you have to put up with. In one way or another, I have been involved with numerous companies that have gone public, including taking Runway Growth Finance Corp.

public in the fall of 2021. (More detail about that in Chapter 19 from me and Runway's CFO, Tom Raterman.)

The fact that the IPO process is a lot of work and less than fun is not a reason to avoid an IPO. However, I do think it's good to be aware of the realities around something that has a lot of mystique and aspiration attached to it. Although many founders dream of taking their company public, it's not always the best solution. There are plenty of people who have it in their mind that they won't have "made it" or truly succeeded unless they do an IPO, which isn't true.

**Being a public company is an enormous amount of work.** The paperwork related to reporting and the disclosures alone are enormous, and you have to make sure you meet the listing requirements, financial and otherwise, of either the NASDAQ or the NYSE.

## Alternative Exits

As great a goal as an IPO may seem, it's not always the best option. And it may not ever present itself as an option. If you have a novel, disruptive technology, you'd probably be an acquisition target early on. An offer would most likely come from either a competitor or a strategic buyer who decides it's cheaper to buy you now rather than later.

### For Tiny and Its CEO, a Big Change

Andrew Roberts had always hoped that his startup, Tiny (now TinyMCE), would be acquired. He describes the acquisition, which occurred in late 2022, as "opportunistic," as the company was looking to raise another round of funding. Andrew's wait for an exit was longer than average: Tiny had been in business independently for 22 years; Andrew served as its CEO for 18.

"Just before we signed a letter of intent to be acquired we were about to be wired several million dollars in venture debt," he recalls. Tiny first raised institutional backing in 2018 from VC firm Blue Run Ventures. "There's quite a lot of growth equity firms sniffing around companies about our size — in the $5 million–$10 million revenue range — because there are a lot of good returns to be made in that part of the market."

He describes the deal as opportunistic because he notes that "the market tanked" after Tiny signed the letter of intent to be acquired in December 2021. "We wouldn't have gotten the same market valuation had we waited."

For his part, Andrew is happy to put aside the risks of remaining independent and the "burden and responsibility" of being CEO, although he remains president. "I'm ready for a little time to revive and recharge and to be more of an individual contributor," he admits. "I'll roll forward a lot of my equity in this new business, so I'm obviously motivated to see it succeed."

Is it worth selling when your goal has been to go public? It depends. You could sell at a discount to where you think you might be in a year, but on the other hand, you could end up with stock in a much larger company that has a long and prosperous future ahead of it.

Many companies turn down buyers because they believe that they can always sell later, but you can't count on it. You especially can't count on being able to do it at a specific time. For example, you could be successful and double the size of your business in one year only for the stock market to decline, which would mean that valuations for comparable companies would decrease. Those deflated comparables would also deflate the value of your company, making it worth less than it was a year earlier.

You might be able to wait out the market, but if you have investors looking for liquidity or lenders looking to be paid back, you won't have the luxury of time.

In my experience, when you look at the risk versus the reward of selling now versus later, more often than not selling sooner rather than later would be the better alternative. There are exceptions, of course, to the idea that selling early is the better choice. Google (now Alphabet), Netflix, Facebook (now Meta), and Dropbox all turned down offers to be bought early on.

If your startup is more about disrupting an existing marketplace or offering incremental improvements on an existing technology/idea, you need to build scale before it's sellable. I would encourage you to create relationships with partners early on, because they'll be among the people most interested in buying you.

Such relationships can also add value to a potential deal. Let's say you hire an investment banker when you're trying to sell your company. The banker (or someone on their team) would probably call some of your customers/partners. Knowing that your technology/product/service is essential to another company's operations makes your company more interesting to a potential buyer.

Private-equity firms also acquire companies, but usually not early-stage companies. For example, investment funds managed by Apollo Global Management acquired 90% of once-mighty Yahoo! in 2021 from Verizon, which had acquired it in 2017.[1] Other PE buyers active in acquiring venture-backed companies include Silver Lake, Thoma Bravo, Vista, and Francisco.

## On Their Radar

How do you become an M&A target? There's a good chance that if your company is on a trajectory where going public would be a possibility and you are building a business of consequence in your specific space, you're already on the radar of investment bankers who operate in your industry.

If you had hoped to go public when you reached $100 million in revenue, they'll probably know about you when your revenues are at less than $50 million. And they'll probably seek you out, even if just to get to know you. A good rule of thumb is that if you don't have any bankers in your contact list, you're probably not ready to go public.

I always encourage entrepreneurs/founders to meet with bankers if the opportunity arises, even if they can't imagine ever selling their company – or buying one. First of all, you never know. Personal circumstances and goals change over time. Secondly, bankers tend to have both good connections and a wealth of knowledge, and it could be useful to you to be able to tap into those resources at some point. Third, as is the case in most situations, you don't want to go looking when you're in need.

---

[1]https://en.wikipedia.org/wiki/Yahoo (accessed August 17, 2022).

Even though many founders – and their teams, especially those who joined early on – dream about going public, if your company is healthy, there is no stigma attached to being acquired. Quite the opposite. Look at all the excellent companies – some of which have gone public, others that hadn't – that have been acquired by big players, with positive outcomes. Those that were acquired before IPO include YouTube, Instagram, WhatsApp, and Nest. Notable post-IPO acquisitions include Netscape, LinkedIn, Fitbit, and Slack.

It's not uncommon to see companies go through the effort of putting together a registration statement for filing with the SEC and going through much of the rest of the process to go public and then get an M&A offer. There's nothing wrong with having worked toward your dream of an IPO and waking up and realizing that your dream has a 2.0 version. Either way, the exit won't come quickly. According to Statista, founders will wait an average of 5.7 years before an exit. For companies that exit for more than $100 million, it takes 11 years – almost twice as long.[2]

## Liquidity versus Liquidation

What a difference just a few letters make. An IPO or M&A is known as a liquidity event where you and your investors will likely get money (in the case of an IPO, you will need to wait for the lockup to expire before you can sell shares). If your company is liquidated because the business is closed due to it's not being able to meet its financial obligations and its assets are distributed to claimants, you'll likely end up with nothing, and your investors, if they are lucky, will see a small return on their investment.

Liquidating a company is not the same as dissolving one. A dissolution is typically a voluntary legal closure of a business, whereas a liquidation involves the selling of a company's assets in order to pay creditors. Dissolving a company through the process of dissolution often takes place when a company is solvent but is no longer actively doing business. Liquidation, however, occurs due to a company having financial difficulties and therefore being unable to keep up with its debts.

---

[2]https://openviewpartners.com/blog/idea-to-ipo-milestones/ (accessed December 11, 2022).

The most common ways for a company to go bust are either for assets to be sold, often for pennies on the dollar, or through a deal known as an "acquihire." The latter would be good news, at least for your employees. These types of deals are specifically structured to keep the employees.

Although we haven't seen companies melt down at the alarming frequency that they did during the dot-com bust, it still happens. Quibi, Solyndra, Jawbone, and BetterPlace are just a few once-promising companies that are no more.

While I think that unsuccessful exits are more about poor execution and strategy than anything else, I also agree with what Touraj Parang says in his excellent book *Exit Path: How to Win the Startup End Game.*

Parang writes, ". . . there is much each and every entrepreneur can do today to pave a viable exit path for their startup. The opposite is also true. Lack of planning today will most certainly hurt their prospects in the future, resulting in a sale at the wrong time to the wrong party, and/or on poor terms, and that's for the lucky few who are able to sell at all before having to turn the lights off permanently. Therefore, building a viable exit path is not just practical, but also an existential imperative for all entrepreneurs regardless of the stage of their startups."[3]

Set yourself up for success rather than wait to be subject to circumstance.

## Key Takeaways

- There are numerous ways to exit: IPO and being acquired are the most common for successful companies.
- IPO may be the dream of most founders, but it's not always the best alternative.
- Your plan for your exit may change, but you should have one from the start.

---

[3]Touraj Parang, *How to Win the Startup End Game* (McGraw-Hill, 2022), 7.

# Part Four

## Making the Best Use of Your Money

# Chapter 13

## Bullshitters, Liars, and Jerks

There are three kinds of people we don't want to be in business with – and I think that's true for most people, regardless of which side of the deal you are on. They fall into three basic categories: bullshitters, liars, and jerks. Every so often you'll come across someone who has characteristics of each.

In this chapter, I'm going to tell you what each of these looks like from our side (the investor's side) of the table. In the next chapter, I'll look at it from your side: what bullshitters, liars, and jerks look like to founders.

### Bullshitters

Bullshitters can be spinners, exaggerators, and even entertainers. Bullshitters, especially the entertaining ones, often don't even know they're doing it – it's just who they are.

It's not uncommon in the startup world for CEOs to try to hide their weaknesses and disappointing results, expecting to overcome them later. This is about spinning/exaggerating. If someone does this – which I consider a form of bullshitting – they have to make sure they don't cross the line to telling outright lies.

This practice of sweeping issues under the rug (in the hopes of fixing them before anyone knows the difference) is common in the world of small, private, venture-backed companies because it's easy to hide issues. After all, the CEO controls everything, there is no one looking over their shoulder, and at this stage, they're probably not getting audited.

For one quarter, a CEO might think, "Oh, well, we'll make it up next quarter." And then they need to hide it a little more the next quarter and again the next quarter (we're up to concealing weaknesses for three quarters at this point), and then pretty soon they're living with a pile of lies they can't get out from under. Things can be hidden during monthly or quarterly board meetings; however, time has a way of turning a small issue into a big one.

I'm not entirely unsympathetic to CEOs in this circumstance. I get that they don't want to expose the board/investors to their failings or shortcomings, especially if they think they'll make it up "soon." But, more often than not, that doesn't happen. Think of it like a little white lie that snowballs and eventually causes an avalanche.

If you're venture-backed, don't think because it's easier to hide issues in these circumstances that you should give it a try. The damage to your reputation and your relationship with directors isn't worth the risk. Boards have a fiduciary responsibility and if they find out you are deliberately misleading them, it's highly unlikely your board will tolerate it.

Some bullshitters are the type who always seem like they're trying to sell something, but never quite firm up the details. After a little while it becomes clear that they're wasting everyone's time. Savvy investors walk away before losing anything other than time. But losing time is no small thing. Once I've been bullshitted about a deal, I'm not going to allow that person to take my time going forward.

The other type of bullshitter is someone who's actually quite charming and fun to be around. They don't go as far as the first type in trying to convince people of something, and I find that these people are often quite creative, if somewhat abstract.

Once, we had a signed term sheet and were in due diligence when we learned more that caused us to be cautious about the opportunity. It wasn't a giant smoking bomb, but a series of things. When you find discrepancies – some minor, some big – you start to feel like you're being BSed.

We decided that the situation was too risky for us. They were nice, fun, awesome guys to go have a drink with – which is often the case with bullshitters – but I didn't want to do business with them.

## Liars

Liars are malicious, purposeful, calculated, and aware. Any investor or lender of note is going to perform due diligence before they invest or lend money. And if someone is a liar – is blatantly dishonest, has a reputation for it, or has lied to get where they are now – this will probably come out in the due diligence process. But not always. Even after 25 years in the startup world, I've been fooled.

In fact, we were fooled at Runway on one of our early loans. After less than a year into the relationship, it became clear that the CEO was a liar, and he wasn't lying just to us. He was lying to everyone at the company – including his board members who were investors.

He blatantly and fraudulently overprojected the company's anticipated sales, presenting an overaggressive plan to the board that they accepted. To us, his lenders, he positioned the software that the company was selling as mission-critical to his clients, saying they couldn't operate their businesses without it. Although he was CEO, he also functioned as the senior salesperson and controlled the communications with all customers. He consistently exaggerated to customers and potential customers the features and functionality of the company's product.

When it became clear that the projected sales were illusory, the board fired the CEO and convinced one of the independent directors to take his place. That board member turned CEO managed the workout in a very satisfying way. When a deal has gone bad, lenders are concerned with losing principal. They have two choices: foreclosing and selling the assets or being patient and letting the team try to turn things around. In this case, the new CEO and I worked closely together. He was the complete opposite of the former CEO: transparent, a consummate professional, and a genuinely good human being.

Even a seemingly small lie can be costly. I recall a situation where we were preparing to close a loan when the background check on the CEO showed that he had committed a felony in college. If this person had told us upfront, it probably would have been okay. As felonies go, it was relatively minor – having to do with a dispute between college roommates over who owned a stereo. The fact that he lied on his application about the felony was something we couldn't live with.

The moral to the story for entrepreneurs: don't lie, because eventually you're going to get found out. The house of cards will come tumbling down, and it's a small enough community that most people aren't going to want to work with you.

Paul Schaut says you always should be able to pass what he calls "the red-face test," meaning that if you see somebody who you dealt with in the past, can you feel good about seeing them and talking to them, or will you get flushed with embarrassment? "The problem is some people don't even have the common decency to get red-faced, and that is its own problem," says Paul. "Those are also people you don't want anything to do with."

## Bullshitting versus Lying

You might ask, where is the line between bullshitting and lying? It's a fair question. Many people exaggerate their accomplishments, the promise of their product or service, the number of people who are potential customers or investors, and so on.

Bullshitters are hoping that people will believe them, but they generally don't get themselves in so deep that they can't find their way out. Liars, on the other hand, may start out knowing the truth but have no regard for it, and can be very adept at eventually convincing themselves – and sometimes stakeholders – of the "alternate reality."

Before we get to jerks, let me tell you that liars and bullshitters are two of the reasons I insist on having contracts reviewed thoroughly by lawyers for both sides.

### And Then There Are the Losers

There is actually a fourth category we don't want to do business with: the losers. In Silicon Valley, there is this big thing about failing: failing forward, learning from failure, being motivated by failure. There is a lot of validity to the idea of not being afraid of failure and there is a lot to be said for businesses that do a lot of small experiments, and learn quickly, and cut off the ones that just aren't working.

> The people who adhere to those ideas aren't who I am talking about. When I talk about losers, I mean the people who repeatedly demonstrate poor decision-making, bad management, or general fecklessness resulting in bad outcomes.
>
> That is the category that is pretty dangerous.
>
> As a lender focused on very-late-stage businesses, Runway doesn't come across losers very often. Our average portfolio company does more than $50 million in revenue. If you were the founder and you built this company, taking it from $0 to $50 million in revenue, you're obviously not a loser.

## Jerks

No surprise, jerks and liars are often flipsides of the same coin. Jerks are mean, contemptible, detestable people. They don't believe in win–win. They can be cruel, rude, or small-minded and are often self-centered and demeaning to others.

Being a jerk can also speak to serious character flaws. Says Paul Schaut, "I had a situation where a key individual was not moral – they were devious and their only goal in life was to be sneaky and get one over on you. And when you deal with people like that, you have to match them with the same level of scrutiny as you apply to the words in the contract."

Paul points out that someone like this is not likely to feel bound by a contract. "It's really hard to have a trusting working relationship if you're relying solely on meticulous attention to the words in a contract to protect yourself because you know that the person on the other side is seeking to get one over on you." I agree 100%.

There was a situation where we had made a loan but as the deal was closing, we were starting to have serious second thoughts about the CEO. He was rude and disrespectful to us and his team, and it got even worse after he got the loan. We were afraid that he would treat clients and partners the same way, which was a real concern, given that he was responsible for negotiating contracts with large companies.

Although he had been successful so far, we didn't want to work with someone whose behavior was so toxic that it could impact the value of his business and the security of our loan.

When it came time for him to seek another round of debt, we suggested that he find another lender, which he did.

The lesson for us was to pay more attention to how someone treated us and their employees. Being a jerk has the potential to negatively impact how your business could grow.

I don't want to give you the impression that I think the startup community is some kind of cesspool of bad behavior, or a magnet for people with enormous personality flaws. Most of my interactions with founders, CEOs, VCs, and other members of the community have been positive.

That doesn't mean that everyone is a saint or that I want to be best friends with everyone. As Kyle Wong points out, "The alignment of incentives and goals, and the interconnectedness of the startup community, especially in a place like Silicon Valley, helps police some of the bad behavior." That's good enough.

## Key Takeaways

- There are three kinds of people investors and lenders don't want to be in business with: bullshitters, liars, and jerks.
- Failure isn't what makes you one of these; lack of honesty, transparency, humility, or failing to meet your obligations will make you one.
- "Life is long. Business is longer." Your reputation will follow you, so be careful.

# Chapter 14

## Bullshitters, Liars, and Jerks, Part 2: What *You* Need to Be on Guard For

Just as lenders and investors don't want to do business with bullshitters, liars, or jerks, you as a founder don't want to, either. You shouldn't have to. And you just shouldn't, period. You may be intimidated by their perceived power or swayed by your desire or need for funding, but I hope that doesn't make you compromise your standards. And as I said in the previous chapter, most of the people I've come across are honest and well-intentioned. But here's some help in avoiding the few that aren't.

### Bullshitters

Bullshitters can be charming and entertaining. They're embellishing the truth more than blatantly telling lies. A general rule of thumb is to assume that someone who is trying to sell you something may be exaggerating in some fashion to be more appealing to you.

This is where you have to put your network to the test and try to find out something about this person's reputation. If you're talking to a potential investor, find out if they eventually come across with the funds. Do they have a reputation for delivering term sheets that differ vastly from the details you discussed? Do they have the connections they say they do? Anyone who advises you to be less than forthcoming or to misrepresent things is someone to avoid.

Bullshitters are less likely to harm you than liars are. Whether they fall on the spectrum of exaggerating rather than being completely full of shit, your biggest loss will probably be time – which, granted, is no small thing, but it won't be fatal.

## Liars

With potential lenders and investors, be wary of anyone who doesn't have a social media presence (what are they hiding?), won't give references (again, what are they hiding?), or gives references and/or tells stories that don't check out. Granted, nobody offers a reference that they think is going to slam them, but you want to go below the surface on references. If they say they've worked with a company but don't explicitly offer them as a reference, there is nothing wrong with checking with the company yourself.

If you've already taken VC money, you probably have someone on your board you can look to for some advice and intelligence. If you've worked with a lender, they ought to be of some use here as well. Even if they haven't worked with a particular company, most likely they have their ear to the ground.

Things to be aware of that an investor or lender may be lying about include not having any money to invest or lend, hiding a history of being a bad partner, or simultaneously looking at an investment in one of your competitors. Also be cautious of someone who changes jobs frequently, or any firm that has a lot of employee churn.

The danger in the scenarios I've outlined here is that you will invest time and energy and won't get the money you hoped for. You've wasted valuable time, and there's the opportunity cost of not having sought out other sources of capital or entertained other offers. Still, I think that is a better outcome than getting mixed up with a less-than-honest provider.

An investor who "encourages" – either tacitly or explicitly – you to misrepresent things is one to avoid. Backers sometimes have unrealistic expectations for growth and when those aren't met, they might push you to paint a rosier picture than circumstances warrant. This should be a red flag in and of itself, but it suggests that they are in turn overpromising to their partners (within their VC firm) and to potential future investors.

Making unrealistic assurances about performance (past and future) benefits no one. It may initially create more VC interest, but it won't end well. In fact, it could play out that the disappointing reality results in you losing your job. Bottom line: don't let investors pressure you to promote an exaggerated business plan.

Even though this chapter is being written for the benefit of founders and CEOs, I think it's worth telling a story about my experience with lying sponsors because of how such a situation could impact you. A private equity firm was looking to sell an underperforming asset and went out of its way to make it look better than it did.

We had made a loan to the company that was being shopped around. The sponsors tried to sell the company behind our back before we knew about the problems. It turned out that prospective buyers saw through the whitewash, and it was impossible to sell the company. When the PE firm couldn't get a price that would allow them to see any proceeds from a sale, they just walked away and gave us the keys.

If anyone asks you to lie, it means that they think lying is okay, and there's a good chance they are lying about something themselves.

## Transparency Is Essential

Sweeping something under the rug and hoping nobody finds it is not going to work in today's world. It's just too easy to find things out. I am not a bullshitter, liar, or jerk, and my belief in transparency is such that I share the fact that because of my service on public boards, I have been named as a defendant in numerous shareholder lawsuits.

Pretty much every single merger and acquisition transaction that gets announced involving a public company triggers a lawsuit in which lawyers for the plaintiffs contend that there was a disparity between value and price – one side is paying too much, or the other side is settling for too little, money. It comes down to saying that the board didn't do its job; ergo, the board members get sued.

These lawsuits are usually a complete scam. I promise you, if Jesus Christ, Allah, Yahweh, and Brahma were on the board, there would still be a lawsuit. And such lawsuits usually get settled just because it's easier, frankly. But as frivolous and unfounded as these lawsuits are, they still are part of a legal action and a matter of public record. In the course of raising money for Runway, I disclosed the fact that I had been a defendant in multiple such lawsuits. More than one investor initially freaked out about it.

That lawsuit issue is now one of the first things I bring up with investors conducting due diligence on Runway. I don't want there to be any suggestion that I withhold pertinent information. And people recognize that my situation is not unique and comes with the territory of being a board member of a publicly traded company.

Certain issues are black and white, and there are definite reasons to avoid doing business with someone. But do your homework and apply critical thinking to a situation that may be nuanced, such as the one I've just described. If the situation were reversed, I would not have a problem doing business with the other party.

## Jerks

Jerks are easy to spot. They're rude, disrespectful, full of themselves (an unattractive quality even if they "have the goods"), and are people you wouldn't want to spend time with as part of your personal life.

Does it ever make sense to do business with a jerk? Ideally, no, but in truth, certain situations may require it. One example might be when you sell your company and the executive leading the effort for the buyer is a jerk.

Perhaps you're going public, and you don't like someone from one of the banks you're dealing with. Sure, you believe the person is honest, and in an IPO, with SEC oversight, there is no room for bullshitting. A "once in a lifetime deal" may justify dealing with a jerk to enable a transaction that will change the lives of your team (and make your investors very, very happy).

As a CEO, you need to be mindful of the example you're setting by who you choose to do business with. If you tolerate a jerk on your team, you're helping to build a less than positive culture. If you tolerate dishonesty from one person, why should everyone else behave with integrity and honesty?

## Key Takeaways

- Bullshitters, liars, and jerks exist on both sides of a deal, so don't be fooled or intimidated by the idea that someone has a lot of power.
- Do your due diligence on people you're looking to be in business with to make sure they're not one of the above.
- Never tolerate lying – from either outsiders or your team.

# Chapter 15

## Your Team: Getting the Right People in the Right Jobs

This is not a management or leadership book; I'm not going to tell you how to build a team and get the most out of it. There are plenty of good books and other sources of information out there, and I list some that I have found useful in the Appendix. But there are several ways in which your team or the structure of it can affect your company financially, so that's the perspective from which I'll be looking at it.

There are three costly team-related mistakes that we often see: too much turnover, hiring too fast, and being penny-wise and pound-foolish when it comes to financial talent. Most of our lending is done to later-stage companies, so these mistakes have already been made – and the damage done.

Companies that come to Runway are still in business, so the mistakes weren't fatal – for them. There are undoubtedly hundreds of venture-backed companies for which at least one of these mistakes contributed to their demise. I'm hoping to help you avoid them, or at least mitigate their potential damage.

### Too Much Turnover

One of the first things we look at when evaluating a company is employee churn. Employee turnover, especially among the engineering, sales, or executive teams, is a real red flag. It suggests that either you have bad judgment when it comes to hiring, or there's something wrong with your culture that makes it difficult for you to retain people. Constantly having to hire people is not only a distraction, but it's expensive in terms of lost productivity and momentum.

If you've experienced a lot of turnover, think about the reasons people leave. People who take jobs in startups expect to work long hours, so anyone who offers that as a reason probably isn't being candid. If you're not asking people why they leave, resolve to start doing that. Talk to someone on the team with long tenure. What have they observed? What have they heard from other employees?

This is a circumstance where your board, or at least one board member, should be able to step in and be helpful. Ask someone on the board to assist with recruitment and hiring. Consider whether you need an onboarding process.

A culture problem is easy to diagnose, but hard to fix. We had an experience with one potential borrower that, on the surface, was the picture-perfect tech company, right down to the foosball table and the beer tap in the kitchen of their Flatiron loft in Manhattan's Silicon Alley. We quickly learned that behind the scenes it was a mess. For one thing, the story didn't match the board decks, which described executive infighting; challenges establishing, prioritizing, and achieving objectives; and difficulty managing temperamental engineering talent.

Employees should feel good about the work they do, the conditions under which they do it, and the people with whom they work. Happy employees are more productive employees. They don't have to love each other and be best friends, but respect, honesty, and collegiality among your team are essential.

If all you're focused on is whether people produce, that's a problem. It's tempting to think, "We've got brilliant people, they're each going to do their job, and this will all just work out." My experience is that things don't just magically fix themselves. Highly skilled talent is in demand, so there's little incentive for unhappy people to stick around.

Venture-backed firms typically don't hire a head of HR soon enough. From my experience, I would say that most companies wait until maybe the fifth or sixth year. Trust me, I'm not a huge advocate of hiring a head of HR too soon. But from "Day One," you should be codifying practices and processes, which are the foundation of a culture. Remember, "culture" is simply another way of saying "the way we do things around here."

Just as it's never too early to think about your exit, it's never too early to think about your culture – building it, nurturing it, and preserving it. If you are the founder and/or CEO, the culture should reflect your beliefs.

Culture is becoming increasingly important as a distinguishing characteristic for companies, so having a strong and positive culture can help you attract and retain the best people, which will certainly impact your company's performance.

## The "Need for Speed"

I always wonder if that phrase should have a question mark in it. Is it necessary for companies to grow at the pace that VCs often encourage them to? Not if growth comes with the cost of making poor decisions.

At a company's earliest stages, you don't have anything to sell, so the focus isn't on revenue growth but on developing your product or service and in assembling the team. You might be too fast to bring on a VP of sales or a chief technology officer, confusing speed with efficiency.

I would say that the more common hiring mistake is hiring on the sales side too soon. You think that to win you've got to sell whatever it is you have – which, of course, ultimately is true – so the logical mistake is thinking you have to get a first-class head of sales.

Your new head of sales will almost always come with a predisposition about how the world works, based on their experience in their previous companies. They'll assume that what worked before is going to work again, and you'll start spending money in that direction. But that might not be the right strategy for your company, and you can end up wasting valuable time and money.

Runway lends mainly to late-stage companies that have already figured out their sales strategy (our average company has more than $50 million in revenue). Typically, that sales mistake is not something that we're seeing them make, but we can see the effects of it. It's like looking at the rings of a tree; you can see when there was a fire, even if the tree now appears healthy.

Your focus should be on developing product, which means putting your money into creating the technology. That means engineers, not a CTO. You could end up with high-priced talent that doesn't really have a job to do yet.

## Making the Money Count versus Counting the Money

Finally, you need to think about the quality of your financial team. Unfortunately, it's usually one of the last places that startup companies invest, which is a mistake. There are now enough different engagement models that companies can get world-class financial talent with decades of experience in increments that are less than full-time.

Too often, people think a CFO is just a glorified accountant and don't understand the value a CFO can add. An accountant is tactical; a CFO is strategic. "I see a lot of entrepreneurs who say that they can get by with an accountant," says Kelly Anderson. She is the founder and CEO of CXO Executive Solutions and works as an interim or part-time CFO. "My favorite is when they say their tax accountant can put the books together. No, that's not the same. Plus, everything they're advising you is on a tax basis, and that's not how you should be managing your business going forward."

A CFO needs to be able to understand exactly what is happening day to day, be able to understand the implications of little decisions on future cash flows, and be there to dot the i's and cross the t's as you go. Their true value is in their impact on strategic thinking.

### Solving for X

Kelly Anderson, founder of CXO Executive Solutions, says she named her company because as an interim CFO, you're solving a problem. It just may not be the one the company thinks it is. "One of the reasons I like doing interim CFO work is you go in and solve a problem", she says. "By the time they need you on an interim basis they're bringing you a problem, but it's really the symptom of the root of the problem."

She says that by the time the problem percolates up, entrepreneurs don't understand the breadth or the depth of the problem. "I do a lot of work trying to help entrepreneurs get the right team in place, including a CFO – and discussing with them how they add value, because the biggest problem you get on the entrepreneur's side is they see it as a cost center."

They often also think a CFO's role is to close the books and provide a financial statement. "That's a controller," she emphasizes. "You want to get to that level of the strategic CFO who's a business partner who asks the right questions: Where do you want to go? How do we get there? Who's our best partner? How do we grow? Where do we allocate our capital?"

Thinking about those questions – and providing strong answers – is usually not part of the entrepreneurial skill set, she says. "Most entrepreneurs are not that great at that. They think they are, but they're really not."

Helping entrepreneurs see that is also part of a CFO's job, she says. "Do you have what it takes to stand up and say, 'Hey, you guys really need to look at this'? There are a lot of CFOs who don't do that."

In the startup world, where "growth at any cost" was a common mantra, investors want the top line to grow as fast as possible. From the VCs' perspective, they don't see a CFO adding to top-line growth. They see stimulating sales as the most important way to add value. Also, they may be managing dilution in not advocating for hiring a CFO. I would argue that if you have a smart, strategic financial partner, they can add significantly to the value of the company – and help protect that value.

Kelly Anderson points out that having a CFO can be highly additive if you're looking for new investors or going through a transaction, getting you higher multiples with "nominal dilution." A CFO will make sure your books and records are complete and in order, knowing and understanding where the costs are coming in, and where to either cut or grow. "You've had somebody that's poked holes in your financial projections so when potential investors talk to you, you will be able to answer all the diligence questions," she says.

"Imagine that you're looking a multiple of two for your business. Get a CFO in there and you can get a multiple of three or four, for anywhere from 2% to 5% equity. I know it happens because I've done it."

It's astounding how many companies, even at the stage at which we invest, have shockingly underinvested in their financial organization. As a company, Runway Growth learned the hard way about what can happen when a company doesn't have a strong finance function. With one of the first companies we lent to, we identified immediately that the guy running finance wasn't up to the task. While performing our due diligence we found pretty serious mistakes. He was an adequate VP of finance but not a CFO.

We pointed it out to the VCs and the CEO and their response was "Well, we know he's not the best, but we're not at the stage where we can afford someone better." We concluded that the rest of the organization was strong enough and their business interesting enough that we would go forward, and we also advised them to get a real CFO.

Very soon after our loan closed, they wanted to make an acquisition. We warned them that for a small company, making an acquisition is often disastrous. They just don't know what they're doing, and in this deal, there were a number of other complicating factors (not the least of which was that the target company wasn't headquartered in the United States, but in a country with a lot of regulations around such deals).

They assured us that their VP of finance could handle it, so, passport in hand, off he went. He completely botched the deal in multiple different ways. (To go into detail would almost be its own book.)

His lack of knowledge and expertise very nearly put the company we had lent to out of business. If it were not for a world-class CEO and a very stubborn, deep-pocketed VC who continued to put in money, and us lending additional money and being very patient, they would have gone out of business.

Why did we lend more money – not once, but twice? A lot of it had to do with the credibility of the main VC and the CEO. I knew and respected both. They had strong track records and a reasonable plan to right the ship and turn a sow's ear into a silk purse. They and the rest of the board realized the mistake they had made and soon after hired a real CFO, on a part-time basis.

A portion of a really good person's time is much more valuable than the full-time efforts of a less experienced person.

By the time you take your first institutional money, you should have a world-class financial person associated with the business. You don't need someone working for you full-time, unless you're in fintech or a business where the financial model essentially *is* the business. In those circumstances, you should have someone who can sit at that table with you, especially when you're talking with investors. By the time you take on debt, you must have that person, even if on a part-time basis. Not having access to strong financial expertise early on is very shortsighted.

We've turned away companies that have a weak finance organization. Without a strong finance function, lenders have a lot less comfort about the accuracy of historical financial information and less confidence in the financial projections. Also, new investors will likely be worried about mistakes – both errors in judgment and not having the facts right – in the past and in the future.

In one case where we came close to making a bad decision by overlooking the weakness of the finance person, I'm pretty sure the CEO was being advised – or even pressured – by his board not to hire a CFO. The VC who sat on the board assured me that he himself was good at controls, and that they would go up a level from the current VP of finance after the next round of funding.

A few times, we've issued term sheets that call for the finance team to be upgraded as part of the deal. Incidentally, two of the deals that we did that way brought on temporary CFOs who were women, and in both cases, they were complete rock stars.

But for us to make that kind of accommodation around a new financial organization is rare. There are too many promising deals out there, and life is both too long and too short to take on the aggravation associated with a financially immature company.

Runway has passed on more than a couple of deals where we've had a preliminary agreement with the CEO and then after starting our due diligence with the CFO we reconsidered because the CFO was inexperienced, incompetent, too difficult, or some of each. And frankly, it doesn't reflect well on the CEO.

## Key Takeaways

- Your team can have a strong impact on your finances.
- Three costly mistakes related to team are not focusing on culture, hiring for growth before you're ready, and not investing soon enough in a strong financial person.
- The financial organization is too often the last place founders invest, and that is both shortsighted and unnecessary.

# Chapter 16

## Founder versus CEO

**B**eing a founder is no guarantee of being a CEO for life – or at least the life of your company. During the past decade, there have been some prominent examples of founders/CEOs with an enormous amount of power thanks to highly favorable stock-ownership arrangements. Probably the most well-known is Meta's Mark Zuckerberg.

It takes two different skillsets to start a company and to run one, and not every founder has it in them to be a CEO, or vice versa. More often than not, it will be your investors who make the determination whether a founder can go the distance, and you're potentially vulnerable at any stage.

"I'm entrepreneurial, but I'm not an entrepreneur," says Paul Schaut, an eight-time CEO who several times has been put in the role by boards. "If you create an idea, and you go start a company, and put your name on it – that takes a lot of guts. I have more confidence in recognizing other people's ideas and the potential in those ideas and putting my name behind it rather than on it."

### CEO and Founder

"As CEO, if you're making all the decisions, you're probably doing something pretty wrong."

So says Kyle Wong, one of four co-founders of Pixlee TurnTo, and its CEO from its founding until it was acquired by Emplifi in late 2022. Not all CEO/founders have Wong's staying power.

Kyle acknowledges that his situation was not the norm, and he gives much of the credit to his fellow co-founders, who all stayed with the company from founding to acquisition. "That makes us both kind of unique and very fortunate," he says of the guys he started the company with in 2012."Early on – definitely in the pre-seed and seed rounds – it's much more about the team than it is one person."

Eventually it does come down to one person with regard to wooing investors and lenders. "Fundraising is a big part of the job of being a tech CEO," he says. "And that's an area that I was more willing to do, or better at, at the time, even though I personally thought that I had a lot of improvements to make."

He knows that not every founder is cut out to be a CEO. "A lot of founders are really good at intensity. But sometimes they forget about the importance of consistency," says Kyle. "It's one thing to pull all-nighters to release the minimum viable product, and to get ready for a great presentation. But you have to consistently perform over a long period of time."

The quartet continued to function as a tight-knit group right up to the time of the exit. "We still work very closely today with various different decisions," he said several weeks before the acquisition. "I don't think just because I have that certain title, it's my way or the highway."

All of their roles changed over the course of the decade, he says, as the company continued to scale. "We're a smaller part of the overall team as we grow," he points out. "A lot of what we do now is more about enabling others than doing the work ourselves."

In one of his CEO stints, Paul was brought in to replace the CEO, and then three years later, he himself was ousted from the top job. "I saw both sides of the revolving door on that one," he says with a laugh. "The big decisions – raising money, raising debt, firing a CEO – are controlled by the institutional money."

It's not uncommon for investors to make their money contingent on bringing in a new CEO. Sometimes they just don't have faith in the current person. Other times, they're not sure what the problem is at the company and think that changing the CEO is the best place to start. They're not close enough to manage the company so they don't have a handle on the nitty-gritty issues.

Often, they see it as their only option. They can't reach in and fire the VP of sales, and they can't easily force strategy changes. Imagine you're a venture investor in a partnership of other VCs, and you've got a company that's not doing well. Every Monday meeting you're reporting and reporting. Pretty soon your partners say, "Just fire that guy." I think that VCs – and boards that are made up of VCs – are often too quick to fire CEOs just because it's their main mechanism for change. It can be the wrong solution to the wrong problem.

Sometimes the CEOs *are* at fault. Let's say they try to sweep things under the rug for a while in the hopes that the situation will get better. If it doesn't, it's an unwelcome surprise to the board, which causes a loss of trust. Then factor in that the company is not achieving its objectives, and the board will say, "That person's got to go." There's probably an unrealistic hope that a different person will bring in some magic, which they rarely do.

Back in my VC days, I once was responsible for a CEO getting demoted – which for some CEOs is the equivalent of being fired – and it backfired on me. The CEO in question wasn't flashy enough, I thought. He was kind of a nerdy, technical guy, and I didn't think he would inspire confidence when it came to raising money or leading the company to the next stage, which was an IPO or an exit.

He did what he had to do to get the money. Meaning, he said, "I hear what you're saying, I'm probably not the right guy to lead it to the next stage, and I'll really embrace the opportunity to have somebody like that." We went out and hired "somebody like that."

It was a complete cultural mismatch. The new CEO was very much a salesperson, while the company itself was very product- and tech-oriented. And the team – possibly spurred on by the former CEO – more or less mutinied and said, "We want the old guy back. We're not going to work for this guy."

So we had to get rid of the new guy and bring the old guy back. In fairness, he did fine. Goldman Sachs took the company public. While it's true he was never a flashy, articulate leader, he clearly inspired the team. If I had to do it over again, I would have embraced him, let him know that I was behind him – and maybe needed to shore up where he had weaknesses, but not try to force a change.

Paul thinks vigorous succession planning is a more practical approach to replacing CEOs. "Having a good board to support the conversations around succession planning, whether it's an immediate plan or more long term, is a benefit to the CEO and all the stakeholders," he says. He spoke of one company he was working with where the board was in the process of evaluating whether the founder would be the right CEO to take the company public.

"I'm having a conversation with him about whether he wants that and if he knows what that means," says Paul. "I said, 'You've got to be ready to have the conversation with your bankers and your investors or others about if you're the guy to go do this and then if we're going to give going public a shot, you've got to have your successor in sight.'"

There's not a lot of patience when someone isn't able to get the job done, he notes. In another company, he convinced both the rest of the board and the CEO, who was "getting tired," that the best course of action was to give the CEO a 9-to-12-month runway with a formal succession planning process. "If we plan it, we can turn it into a positive," he remembers telling the board. They hired a CRO with the goal of eventually making him CEO, giving him the chance to settle into the company and have an easier transition.

Clint Korver didn't need a board to tell him that he wasn't cut out to be an entrepreneur – despite having founded four companies. "I was an entrepreneur for about 15 years in Silicon Valley and I found out that I was not a very good entrepreneur," he says. "I was great at starting [businesses]. But eventually I realized that I love the intellectual part of starting companies. The very beginning, I would argue, is quite intellectual, because you have to figure out what problem you want to solve. What's the market? How do you create a product? How do you price the product?"

As a seed-stage investor through Ulu Ventures, Clint is now able to follow those intellectual pursuits, and also help advise fledgling companies and their founders. I think he serves as a great inspiration to any founder who either recognizes or has been "told" that their time as a CEO is limited.

If your talents lie in being a founder, keep going! Says Alec Wright, "The first test of every great founder is can you convince one, two, or three of your smartest friends or the people in your network to come in and join this crazy venture of yours?" If you were able to do it once, you can probably do it again. And as Paul Schaut says, there's no greater compliment than people being willing to work with you a second time.

## Key Takeaways

- Being a founder is no guarantee that the CEO job will be yours for as long as you want it.
- Investors often flex their power by having a CEO replaced – which isn't always the solution.
- If your skillset lies in being a founder rather than a CEO, embrace that skillset.

# Chapter 17

## Getting the Most from Your Board

Your board can be a tremendous asset to you as you build your company. Its size, composition, and influence will evolve with your company. At any stage, board members, especially those who become members because of their investment in your company, can help you make smart choices about money: how to source it, best use it, and preserve it. That's why it's critical that you make smart choices about who joins your board.

First you need to understand what a board looks like and how it functions.

### Structure

At the early stages, your board is probably going to be one or two people from your company (likely the first founders), one or two investors, and one independent director that you and the investors find mutually acceptable. Independent directors are usually industry experts who can add value around product development, go-to-market plans, and strategic partnerships or potential exits.

Five is the most common number of board members for an early-stage company. As you go into subsequent investment rounds, one of the board members from your company is probably going to have to exit the board to make room for another investor. At that point, the board will likely be one person from the company (usually the CEO), three investor representatives, and one mutually acceptable independent director.

Not all investors look to sit on boards, especially with the influx of new sources of money flowing into Silicon Valley, but I would advise you to look for investors who will be active and additive.

As funding progresses, there's a good chance your early investors (and the accompanying board members) will get displaced. "I have an agreement with almost all of our entrepreneurs that at the Series A, I'm going to roll off," says Ulu's Clint Korver. "Our thinking is, we're an expert from seed up to Series A. And when someone like a Sequoia comes in further in your series, you're in great hands, and our comparative value-add at that point goes down dramatically."

If you are fortunate enough to have a Sequoia or a Benchmark as an early investor, they won't be replaced as board members, and you wouldn't want them to be. Even if they don't invest additional money, their cachet and gravitas have enormous value. For example, if you tell prospective investors that your lead VC is Sequoia, that will be helpful to you when it comes to raising downstream capital.

The more investors with a representative on the board, the more you need to watch for divisions within the board. And that can easily happen when investor groups have differing agendas.

On the other hand, you don't want board members who are so cozy that you end up with groupthink, or who will automatically vote in lockstep with each other. You want open debate, and people who are willing to air different points of view. Even if everyone ends up in the same place, the journey matters.

A venture debt lender isn't likely to sit on your board. It's too much of a time commitment, and isn't really in keeping with their role. That said, at Runway, if one of our companies needs assistance, we're always available to them.

## Observers

Observers are a special category of board participant, and there is an art to managing them well.

"Observer" is an official status. It can be defined as just participating in the open portion of the board meeting, or as participating in everything from board meetings to serving on committees.

If things get sensitive or it looks like there might be a potential conflict, the observer will be asked to leave the meeting. You want to structure the observer role so that you get the maximum benefit from their involvement – advice, serving as a sounding board, acting as a potential mediator – without the person feeling like a second-class citizen because they don't vote.

An observer likely has some financial stake in the company, but perhaps not enough to justify giving them a board seat. Other reasons to have someone serve in an observer role are that they just don't have the gravitas for a board seat to make sense, or that their company's policy is to not take board seats. That's often the case with corporate investors.

Because an observer doesn't get to vote, they have less direct influence over the direction of the company. Still, you should treat them with respect and make them feel that their service is adding value.

## Lead Director

Once your board gets to be a certain size, you need a director who will function as "lead director" even if they're not formally named as such. If you're following good board governance, after most board meetings, there should be a session just for the directors – meaning no one from management is present. The person responsible for reporting back to management is the lead director.

Now that I'm the CEO of a public company with an independent board, I'm aware of just how valuable the lead director function is – and how important it is to have efficient, open communication. Even if you don't designate a lead director by title, there needs to be an understanding around who is going to be the primary line of communication between the board and the CEO. If you have an independent director who also serves as chairman of the board (as opposed to the CEO being chairman), this person will usually serve as the lead director.

In developing a workable relationship between you and a lead director, you need to balance what to share versus what not to share, and who you can run problems by without running the risk of feeling like you appear weak or that you're failing. There's an art to that, which one can never really master, but I suggest erring on the side of overcommunicating.

The relationship, like any other, will develop over time, and, as always, honesty is the best policy. The CEOs should always be thinking about how they are perceived by their board, and be open to feedback around that.

## How the Board Adds Value

Now that you understand the structure, let's look at the role of the board. Says Clint Korver, "I'd argue the goal of a startup board is to help the entrepreneur learn faster – learn about their business, how to build a scalable model, and learn about their customers."

In addition, board members can offer advice, open doors, help with the next stage of funding, make critical introductions, and bring cachet and connections.

Imagine you're trying to structure or negotiate a corporate relationship with another, better-established company than your own. You can go to your VC board members for help. They may have a person on their team who is dedicated to helping portfolio companies; someone in their firm may have a relationship with the company in question. This is a broad example of how board members add value.

You need to think specifically about what you and your company need.

### The Professional Board Member

Just as all money is not created equal, neither are board members.

Paul Schaut is a former CEO of eight companies – including several where he went from being a board member to being interim CEO – and a professional board member. "I don't want to just show up at board meetings," he says. "I was on one board for eight years where the CEO, who was very smart by the way, didn't want her board members to do anything other than just check the box."

Although that stint was lucrative, Paul decided he had more to offer. He felt he could leverage his years of experience – starting with sales roles in the early days of tech in the 1980s to being a strategic CEO – to be what he calls "an engaged board director." To him, that means spending real time with the company on an operating level.

"I can relate to the investors and to the CEO and to the management team," he says. "I decided that's what I wanted to get paid for beyond just a token quarter of a point of equity."

He quickly went to work on two boards, and 17 years later, he has some 30 board roles under his belt. To him, serving on a board is very different from being the CEO. "There's an ego component to being a CEO – a confidence, a drive, an impatience to make decisions. You've got to put all that away when you go on a board," he says. "I joke with people that if you're a competent CEO, you've got to take a Quaalude before you go into a board meeting because that's not your role."

But having been a CEO allows him to make unique contributions – advising around strategy setting, solving issues, leveraging his network for recruiting, raising money, doing M&A or business development, and sales. Also, "If things are going to hell, the board is going to look to the member that has CEO experience to step in. I've had that happen five times," Paul says. "I bring not only my network and experience, but my scar tissue and lessons learned to these situations."

As a founder, you may face the decision of whether to take an associate from a big-name firm who has never done a venture deal before as a board member. No doubt this person is really smart, but if they've never sat on a startup board before, their ability to add value is likely limited. Part of what makes one firm more attractive than another is the value they bring beyond money.

Would I rather have an inexperienced person from a big-name firm or a more experienced partner from a lesser-known firm? There are too many factors in play for there to be one "right" answer. Let's say a less-well-known firm is pitching you, but they're offering a seasoned person with expertise in your space as a board member. I would argue that you should consider whether a person with great expertise would compensate for any weaknesses on your team. If this potential board member would truly be additive, that could be a strong reason to go with a less-well-known firm.

You also have to think about how much influence the person has within the VC partnership, and what your chemistry is like with the potential board member – and with the other people at the firm.

As with any person you're going to do business with, do as much due diligence as you can, and that should include in-person meetings with any potential board members. Sometimes good people just don't get along, and if you can avoid having someone on your board who you don't feel is a "fit," best to avoid it. But keep the big picture in mind. If you're rejecting someone – and their money – do it for a good reason.

It's important that you and your VC board member(s) have a shared vision for your exit in terms of timing and what kind of exit you're shooting for. VCs, especially the top firms, are usually more focused on the value at which you will exit than the speed at which you do so. Accordingly, VCs care a lot about what percentage of your company they own. (This can work to your advantage in negotiating the valuation of a round, as VCs are often willing to accept a higher valuation if it allows them to invest more and own a greater percentage of the company.) When your vision and the board's aren't in concert, that can lead to problems.

Imagine you've got a good business with a valuation of $500 million, and you and the rest of your management team own 20%. You get an offer to be acquired. Chances are, to you and your team that $100 million could be life-changing. But for some VCs, their share of proceeds wouldn't be interesting enough. They might favor more growth so the valuation would be higher, wait for a better offer, or push for an IPO. This lack of agreement will make life difficult.

Also, consider a circumstance where you raise a late-stage round at a high value (say over $1 billion, making you a unicorn). The new investors want to earn a multiple of at least 2×, so you'll need to exit for at least $2 billion to satisfy them. That might not be consistent with the desires of your management team and early investors, who would prefer to exit sooner, at a value below $2 billion.

Managing divergent interests among your shareholders and board members can be a challenge, and the more complex your cap table, the more difficult the challenge. This is a strong argument for taking debt, as it minimizes such conflicts. And if you're looking at taking debt in the growth stage or late stage, you can avoid giving up high-value equity.

A good VC can help you refine and shape your vision and will most likely be essential to making your vision a reality. It isn't just their money. Their advice, connections, cachet, and experience can be enormously helpful to you. When I was a VC, someone from our firm always sat on the boards of the companies we invested in. We were looking for great entrepreneurs looking for fuel, not only in the form of capital but also help – with strategy, introductions, and offering an experienced confidant with whom to share ideas, challenges, and aspirations.

All that said, you need to remember that founders, not VCs, build companies. VCs are there to help you, but don't get overwhelmed or intimidated by their power. "Our rule of supporting companies is first, do no harm," says Clint Korver. Which is good. "Every entrepreneur, if they're onto something really exciting, is probably doing things differently than people who've done it in the past. So some of the lessons from the past will apply, and others won't." In his view, the entrepreneurs are the only people who can say which lessons apply to them and which don't.

Pixlee's Kyle Wong shares a similar view. "As CEO, you know what is best for your company and it's your duty to educate the board." He makes a good point – the communication and learning need to go in both directions.

What Clint and Kyle say isn't a license to get so cocky that you dismiss the value board members can add, or forget to leverage it. Should that happen, your board members will probably be quick to remind you, and that can create a level of tension that's not necessary or productive. You need each other: VCs make money by investing in companies that become successful; companies become successful by leveraging all the resources made available to them.

## Key Takeaways

- The board composition and structure will change throughout your company's growth.
- Board members offer more than money. You need to leverage their expertise, connections, insights, and wisdom.
- You and your board may disagree, although you should strive for agreement. Even when you don't agree, board members should be viewed as allies.

# Chapter 18

## The Moral Contract

I t's easy to be a great partner when everything's going well. The real test of a partnership is when things aren't going well. By then you're bound to each other, so hopefully you were careful and wise in choosing your partner(s).

One way we at Runway Growth Capital try to differentiate ourselves is by being seen as a strategic partner, not a commodity provider or merely the people on the other side of a transaction. That's important because we very rarely work with companies at the beginning of their financing journey, which means that our journey with a company is likely going to be shorter than a VC's. We have less time to "prove" ourselves and to get to know each other. The shorter duration of our partnership is one of the many reasons we are so careful about maintaining a good reputation and acting by the terms of what we call "the moral contract."

This isn't to be confused with a "morals clause" – a portion of a contract that stipulates that someone is to behave in accordance with a certain agreed-upon standard of behavior, the violation of which will cause a penalty that could include the voiding of the contract. Nor is it the equivalent of what's agreed upon legally by both sides at the start of your relationship. A moral contract is one that you make with yourself and fulfill on behalf of others. I think of it as "What you do to and with your partners that allows you to sleep at night." (I'm using "partners" loosely here, not in the legal sense of partners at a firm or in a business.)

For a founder, the notion of the moral contract probably starts when you take money, whether gifts or investment, from your parents/family and/or your friends. Those are likely the last people in the world whose money you'd want to lose or misuse. A moral contract should guide you throughout your entire journey, but it really only works if all parties share the same view.

When it's time to take money from a VC or a lender, that moral contract is about forging a partnership to take your business to the next level. VCs and lenders try to differentiate themselves on how they can help you build your business and their approach to that. Not every successful VC would be a good fit for every startup or with every founder, nor would every lender.

There are those VCs you'd love to have as investors because their previous successes have made them so famous that just having them invest in you and join your board will have a halo effect. But your selection process should really be viewed as picking a partner, not just finding a source of money.

At the furthest extreme in terms of looking for a partner rather than merely the other party in a transaction is picking a bank. I'm not talking about an investment bank, but a bank that will handle your company's day-to-day business transactions. You don't really need a partner here so much as an institution that has a good reputation and is not going to go out of business.

But when you start borrowing money from either a bank or a nonbank lender like Runway, you can view your lender as a commodity provider – in this case the commodity being money – or as a partner. I think you should look for someone who sees themselves as your partner. That's how we want to be viewed by companies we do business with.

From your end, being a partner means being honest and transparent. On our end, it's about understanding the nuances of your business and your decision making, and looking at your company through an individualized lens.

We lent money to a company called eSilicon where the loan was extended repeatedly. Says former eSilicon CEO Jack Harding, "We were in this unique situation where we needed to work with a shop that had the foresight to understand that the transitions we were going through as a company were going to result in high returns – down the road.

"We felt confident that this was the right decision for our business and we needed someone who could calibrate risk and understand it. And not all the people we approached were equally adept at doing that – or willing to. Runway acted as a true partner."

Flattered as I am by Jack's kind words, I'd be disingenuous if I didn't point out a few things. My reputation mattered to Jack and his did to me, which gave me a certain level of comfort in doing an unusual deal. One of the reasons we were willing to take a larger risk than we usually do is that we performed a rigorous due diligence process – more so than usual, because of the extra risk involved. It ended up paying off for everyone, but it did require patience on our part. We were willing to do so in part because of our due diligence, but also because I knew that Jack and his team at eSilicon saw us as partners.

## The Moral Contract in Action

"We'd hired an investment bank to help us sell eSilicon, because we'd had some incoming interest and the time seemed right for a variety of reasons," remembers former CEO Jack Harding. "The acquiring party we decided to sell to was undervaluing a significant part of the business, which they weren't very interested in."

Jack went back to the acquiring CEO and said, "Look, you're not loving this piece of our business, but I have another guy who would kill to get this asset. Let me sell this piece to them, and I'll split the proceeds with you."

It was an unusual proposal, Jack admits – and I agree. The guy he was selling to said, "Let me get this right. You're going to take this piece that I was going to buy that I admittedly don't love, and you're going to sell it for 10 times more than I am valuing it at to a third party, and we're going to split the proceeds."

Jack said, "Exactly." And the other guy said, "That's very risky, and it's very complicated."

He was right, but Jack was also confident that we could get the deal done because he knew that I had known the guy who wanted to buy the piece of the business for 20 years – way before my time at Runway. This three-party deal dragged out the primary deal by several months. Against the advice of all the lawyers and the directors of both eSilicon and the company that was buying the rest of the business, Jack came to Runway Growth. The deal was explained to me as "eSilicon has a chance to optimize value for everybody, but it's going to take more time to get three parties to agree than it would to get two."

I was intrigued by both the value proposition and the value generation and agreed to be patient while we set out to perform this "triple lindy." "Runway gave us relief and forbearance on our debt so that we could close the sale, even though Runway had the right to sweep our accounts to get their money back," says Jack.

Not all borrowers will recognize the distinction between a true partner and a provider. As I was writing this book, Runway decided not to lend money to a company with whom we had a signed term sheet. As we were performing the last stages of due diligence, we just didn't feel that they viewed us or respected us as a partner. We got the sense that they just saw us as a bag of money and felt they would have no qualms about lying to us or screwing us over.

Before we close a deal, we tell people how they can expect us to interact with them – and how we expect them to interact with us. Sometimes I think of founders as pro athletes. They're extremely gifted but need the discipline and boundaries that come from being coached and recognizing that they are part of a team. It's also critical that they understand the rules of the game.

Just because I am a believer in the moral contract doesn't mean I don't care about written ones. I am a stickler for documentation when it comes to making deals. Some people like to think of themselves as handshake people. I'm not one of them. Sometimes those people are genuine and trustworthy, but I've been burned too many times.

As counterintuitive as it might seem, the closer the relationship, the more important documentation is. With a close relationship, the stakes are higher and the likelihood of assumptions and misunderstandings being made that can cause trouble is far greater.

I had to borrow money from my best friend at one point (and I'm not talking $50 for beer money in college) and we papered the agreement exactly as we would have – and should have – any other agreement. I'm happy to say that it all worked out – the money was paid back as agreed, and we're still best friends, without any awkwardness between us. I have observed the destruction of countless relationships with family and friends because things weren't documented. From the very first dollar you take from your parents or your pals, write it down!

I can't overemphasize the importance of the relationships that underpin the moral contract. Too often, business is transactional and any sense of connection is fleeting at best. In building a startup, when you're assembling that initial team, not just your first employees but beyond that – your VC(s), board members, and growth lender – it's important that you think of them as part-ners, because the relationships you have with them should not be transactional.

From a VC's perspective, the moral contract isn't so much about what they can do with their own checkbook as it is what they can do with their advice, contacts, and influence. They are investing their reputation in you.

The moral contract helps build and bind a group with the idea of working together to find the best outcome. Ultimately, it may not be what everyone has wished for, but in my experience, it's pretty rare for people to feel that they got the raw end of a deal.

## Key Takeaways

- There are partners and providers. Look for partners.
- A moral contract is a complement to a written one.
- A moral contract won't work if only one side abides by it.

# Part Five

## Going Forward

# Chapter 19

## Runway's Story of Going Public

If you make it to the IPO stage, congratulations! It's more than a testament to your technology, business model, and hard work. It's vindication.

It's also a mixed bag.

At its best, Tom Raterman, Runway Growth Capital's CFO, describes the IPO process as "fun and invigorating." "You're working on something that's monumental for the company that you've been building toward for years," he says. "Assuming the stock trades as expected and the underwriters deliver on their promises, the day you go public can be one of the most exciting days of your life." That's the upside.

It is also tedious and grueling. You have to manage the process and all the parties involved and their wants and needs, while at the same time, paying attention to your business. A negative event – in the market, in the economy, at your company – could derail the IPO process. "It's an exhausting process from start to finish – interviewing and choosing the underwriters, negotiating their positions and roles in the transaction, and determining economics," Tom says of the downside. You have to build and maintain the data room for business due diligence, legal due diligence, and financial models and scenario analysis.

"All of the previous work has to be complete before anything else begins, including drafting the prospectus, developing all the input that goes into the prospectus, making sure that everything's catalogued and mapped and that you've got every piece of data to support every comment, and developing the themes and the story that you want to tell," he continues. "It's like a Rubik's Cube. If you twist one thing, then another one can get out of whack."

The process of going public usually takes six to nine months. That's on top of the 12 months that it will take *to prepare* to go public. "It could take a year to make sure that you've got your financial operations, systems, and statements in place so that they're audit-ready," he points out. There are myriad other internal details to sort out. Some of them won't be terribly complex – just time-consuming and expensive, such as redoing all of your E&O and D&O liability insurance.

As part of your preparation to go public, you have to find the bankers who will underwrite the deal through what's known as a "beauty contest." You're looking at two sides of the bank: the investment banking arm and the research arm, and you need to perform due diligence on the two sides simultaneously. As far as the research analysts go, you have to look at anything they publish about your peers, you've got to talk to them and get to know them, and then decide whether you want to include that institution as being a potential underwriter.

You choose your underwriters for two reasons. One is their distribution and ability to execute on the IPO, which is in the hands of the investment bankers, equity capital markets, and the sales and trading teams. The other is research. You need them to commit to covering you and providing ongoing research.

The fees that go to the underwriters pay for three things: the selling of the initial offering, the immediate post-IPO stabilization process, and post-IPO, long-term support. On the investment banking side, that means keeping you up to date on happenings in the market, and advising on the potential for following offerings and M&As. On the research side, it's writing research reports, organizing nondeal roadshows, and including you in their investor conferences.

Bear in mind that the investment banking side and the research side are separate. But you wouldn't choose an underwriter unless you had spoken with the team from the research side, and vice versa. One side will introduce you to the other side of the house in either a chaperoned call – with the compliance department, where the bankers won't be on the call – or you will have an unchaperoned call with just research. There is a wall between research and investment banking that needs to be respected by all parties.

## A Bright, Sharp Line

Once your company is publicly traded, the quality of the research analysts and their willingness to write about you – to cover you – are critical. The Global Analyst Research Settlement, an enforcement agreement reached in 2003 between the SEC, NASD, NYSE, and 10 of the largest investment firms in the United States, established a bright, sharp line between investment banking and research. As a result of that settlement, a bank's research department decides which companies it will cover, not the investment banking department.

That said, your chances of getting covered by a bank's research arm will likely improve if the investment banking arm has gotten even a small piece of the underwriting pie. Presumably, the research arm provided information that helped the investment bank decide whether to pursue your business.

Post-introductions, the bank will go through an internal process to circle up and see if research is comfortable with the company and the business. If research isn't, it's unlikely that the underwriters will take it on.

For the IPO of Runway Growth Finance (a part of Runway Growth Capital), we put together a list of who we thought were the top bankers in our space and reached out to a group of them, requesting that they make a pitch. All but one participated. We held six 90-minute presentations over a two-day period, listening to these people talk about their capabilities, how they would position us and what they thought our story was, and describe their success in doing IPOs for our peers. We ended up including all the banks that had pitched us in the underwriting. Later in the process, we added two smaller banks.

After the beauty contest is when things usually start getting ugly, with the "winners" jockeying for position and fighting over fees. The gross spread – the financial institutions' profits from the IPO listing – is split a number of ways and the process of allocating those economics among the active bookrunners, the passive bookrunners, and the other managers/participants is important and often difficult. This process will influence who (which underwriter) sells the initial IPO shares.

There is a hierarchy among the underwriters – the different investment banks – who will buy the shares of your company and sell them to the public. The lead underwriter – also known as the lead left underwriter – will be listed above and/or to the left of everyone else on the cover of the prospectus. The lead underwriters drive the due diligence and the valuation process.

The bookrunners determine share allocations for institutional investors (which comprise the bulk of most deals) and receive more of the economics. In addition to taking the primary responsibility for getting your shares to market, they'll assess your company's financials and current market conditions to arrive at the initial value of the company and the number of shares to be sold. They'll manage the overall process, which will likely include forming a "syndicate" of other underwriters.

The hierarchy gets more subtle and nuanced after the lead left position. All of these investment banks are incredibly competitive, and where they rank on a prospectus is very, very important to them. You'll have banks who will flat-out say, "We won't be below such-and-such bank." That is the kind of competitiveness you're seeing with banks of a certain level. The companies are fighting not just for bragging rights but also for the subsequent fees they can make for being the lead left underwriter.

You can have several lead underwriters or joint bookrunning managers. Runway had four, all prominent names. JP Morgan was the lead left, followed by Morgan Stanley, Wells Fargo Securities, and UBS Investment Bank. We also had four other companies as co-managers: Oppenheimer & Co., B. Riley Securities, Compass Point, and Hovde Group LLC. Additional underwriters are usually also allocated shares to sell.

When they are wooing you, investment bankers will say, "We want to do what's best for you," and "We have your company's best interests at heart," but it won't seem that way. They'll also tell you, "It's up to you," suggesting that you hold all the cards, but that's really not the case, because they'll keep on threatening to walk. If you reach the point where you'd consider firing them, it won't be practical, even though it would feel good in the moment.

Banks will also tell you that they need a certain position in the pecking order "to provide their best thinking." All the underwriters will have access to the same information, so any one of them can provide their "best thinking" regardless of their position in the hierarchy.

When you hear them say that, what they're really saying is, "If you don't put us where we want in the ranking (which also means pay us what we want to be paid), you're going to get the B team." Consider yourself lucky to get the B team.

If someone at BlackRock were to read my observations, they would probably laugh and say, "The banks work for us." That's true of BlackRock. Likewise, if you're a Snowflake – one of the hottest IPOs in decades – you can call the shots.

For someone like us, not so much. We did have more indirect influence in our IPO than we might have otherwise because of our affiliation with Oaktree Capital Management, which owns approximately 30% of Runway. Such a situation isn't unique to Runway or Oaktree. Substitute any other company going public for Runway and substitute any other money manager for Oaktree in this equation, and 90% of the time, the same dynamic would play out.

No doubt there are banks and bankers who pride themselves on relationships, and thus are less likely to argue as much about where they rank, fees, and so on. I promise you, though, even the most collegial banks and the ones who know they're not top-tier still have their own archenemy and won't want to be below them.

It's extremely common for banks to threaten to walk if they don't get the fees or the allocation of shares that they want. They'll fight over fees tooth and nail, down to the decimal point. You've got to either call their bluff or let them drop out. Chances are you'll have to rejigger the allocations.

## Runway's Story of Going Public

Preparing for an IPO is – and always has been – filled with a lot of high-pressure pitches, smooth-talking salesmen, and empty promises. The satisfaction of taking a significant step forward for the future of your company can get temporarily lost. I observed this both as an investment banker and as a VC, but I felt it when we took part of Runway public.

Imagine you're getting married, and up until the minute you're walking down the aisle you're negotiating who gets paid more: the officiant or the place where you're having the ceremony. Then all of a sudden, the wedding party wants to get paid – and each person thinks they deserve more than the others. They keep on arguing until some kind of arrangement is made.

That's how I felt in the runup to taking one of the funds managed by Runway Growth Capital, LLC public, which occurred in late 2021. As a founder/CEO, I found the process extremely unsavory.

Before Runway (RWAY) went public, I had been on all sides of an IPO, having started my career in corporate finance as an investment banker helping companies go public. As a VC I've sat on the boards of numerous companies that have gone public and was more closely involved than I was as an investment banker. Thanks to all of these experiences, I was keenly aware of all the requirements, the roles different parties would play, and the steps involved.

None of that prepared me for being at the center of the process. There are a host of decisions to make that aren't related to what you've previously focused on – your strategy, and developing, marketing, and scaling your product or service.

We were told that in order to get a bank's "best thinking," the bank needed to be the lead left underwriter. They didn't end up as lead left underwriter, and we didn't get their best thinking.

I can't overstate how important it is for a niche business to have high-quality research analysts who want to cover you and really understand your industry and your business. In addition to our four lead managers, we had four co-managers when Runway went public in hopes that their high-quality research analysts would cover us.

It was disappointing and deflating that this process was so fraught with what from our perspective seemed so unimportant. It is unseemly for people from some of the biggest, most influential investment banks in the world to fight over a $50,000 fee as if they were toddlers fighting over a toy.

On the other hand, it was thrilling when we actually went public, and I remain proud of this achievement each and every day.

Welcome to Wall Street, everyone.

You can expect underwriters to keep coming at you, discreetly but not so discreetly trying to adjust their position in the pecking order. They'll boast about what they're bringing to the party or diminish someone higher up on the food chain. Any time they ask for a private meeting, it's safe to assume they're trying to improve their position.

For a small company like Runway Growth, in a niche area – venture debt – the role and the efforts of the underwriters were very important. When a deal is so hot that everyone wants to buy the stock, it doesn't matter nearly as much who the underwriters are. An offering in a company that provides venture debt is not the next big thing, and there are a select number of buyers for a stock like ours.

One way to simplify the process and make it less unpleasant is to use one bulge-bracket investment bank and surround it with others that are clearly not on that level. That makes the issue of who will be lead left underwriter quite obvious. The three giants among the premier investment banks are Morgan Stanley, Goldman Sachs, and JP Morgan. Even though Morgan Stanley doesn't cover venture debt, we were more than happy to have them as part of the deal because of their vast distribution capabilities, global credibility, and cachet.

If you are looking for broad retail distribution, there are a few other banks to consider, most notably Wells Fargo and Bank of America. This is not a comprehensive list – there are other banks that are influential and powerful. This list should not be viewed as an endorsement for one institution over another.

## Gating Events

Once you've established your syndicate, there are four significant events that will take place. The first is **analyst day**, when the management team presents a four-hour deep dive on every part of the business to all the underwriters' research analysts. The management team will be introduced to the analysts so they can see the depth and breadth of your team. Up until then, they've probably only known the CEO and the CFO.

There's a lot of preparation behind that presentation: rehearsals where the investment bankers are asking you difficult questions, critiquing you. You provide the analysts with kind of an abbreviated version of your model so that they can build their own forecast models.

The second step is **drafting the prospectus**. That involves developing and gathering all the input that goes into the prospectus, making sure everything's catalogued and mapped, that you have every piece of data to support every comment, and developing the themes and the story that you want to tell. It's a significant amount of work, and it can make or break the success of your offering. You'll settle in on the model, the forecast that you want the Street to have, and set the tone for the analysts to carry forth.

"The amount of work and detail that goes into making sure that those filings are right, to gathering all the information, to handling the due-diligence requests, to arguing over words with the lawyers and the investment bankers and getting back to the SEC with answers that seem obvious or irrelevant – it's all painful," says Tom Raterman. "If you don't have a strong, resilient team, you're not going to get through it."

---

### NASDAQ versus NYSE

Which exchange a company lists on matters very little to most founders. Your shares can be widely traded regardless of whether you list with NYSE or with NASDAQ. That said, the two exchanges act like you're making a religious decision and compete aggressively to win business they think is important. Both exchanges will offer cash and noncash incentives (mostly in the form of marketing support). You can take advantage of this to secure a promise for advertising dollars in support of building your brand.

---

Step three is **testing the waters** – probably three days of presentations to prospective investors. Feedback is consolidated by the bankers, and then a decision is made whether the IPO is a go or not. If you decide it's a go, you're going to print ("print" is figurative because it's done electronically) your red herrings, a preliminary prospectus that is filed with the SEC. They will comment, and after they're satisfied that you've addressed any concerns, they'll sign off on the offering.

Assuming the deal is a go, the **two-week roadshow** is step four. That involves meeting with investors and trying to sell the offering. There will be three groups involved from the underwriters: the investment bankers, the research analysts, and the institutional sales team. They work in concert to set up meetings with known IPO buyers. In pre-Covid times, this was all done in person, starting on the West Coast and ending in New York.

From the investment banking team there will be the relationship team, with whom you will work day to day, and the equity capital markets people, who are the experts on the IPO and equity markets and how deep the market is for your offering. This group works closely with the institutional sales force.

After the roadshow, a final price is decided – which might change right up until the night before the IPO.

Despite all Tom and I have said about how laborious (from his perspective) and unpleasant (from mine) the process is, if an IPO makes sense for you, don't be discouraged or dissuaded from going through with it. Don't lose heart when you are so close to the prize.

## Key Takeaways

- Going public is a long process that takes detailed preparation and can be both daunting and disheartening, so keep your eye on the end result.
- Expect the underwriters to fight among themselves and with you over their roles and the fees they receive.
- You are paying the banks for three things: the original selling process, the immediate post-IPO stabilization process, and post-IPO, long-term support.

# Chapter 20

## Conclusion

When I first thought about writing this book, my plan was to write it mostly, if not exclusively, from the perspective of Silicon Valley proper. That is where much of my experience with venture capital and venture debt has occurred over the past 20 years. But as I began working on the book in earnest I realized that a book of such a narrow focus was not going to be of the greatest service to the startup/founder community.

I would be giving short shrift to the many people who are creating opportunities elsewhere – via online communities and resources, by becoming a part of and helping to build vibrant ecosystems throughout the country, or starting out wherever they can. Also, I didn't want to perpetuate the idea that if you didn't come out of Stanford or Berkeley, you are at a huge disadvantage. That might have been the case 20 years ago, but it certainly isn't any longer.

If anyone questioned whether proximity to Silicon Valley had become less important, whether for founders, VCs, or workers, Covid certainly put those questions to rest. Covid has proven that teams can work remotely, which means companies likely feel more comfortable in hiring remote workers, which can be a boon to the bottom line.

I had started writing this book pre-Covid and then put it on hold as I was working on taking Runway Growth Finance Corp. public. My own perspective on the necessity of working in person changed during that process. As much as I like looking someone in the eye before making a deal, even I must grudgingly admit that little was lost by not doing all of our meetings in person.

This realization caused me to reflect on other changes that have occurred during my time in the Valley, some of which have already been mentioned in the book. There is a greater awareness of venture debt and it is being more wisely and creatively used. As Kyle Wong pointed out, it now factors into funding strategy, being used not only to lessen dilution – still a major selling point of debt – but also to give companies more flexibility throughout their journey to exit.

I believe debt's use will increase as people become not only more aware of it but understand it better as a complementary way of raising money for startups. Just as venture capital is not always the answer, neither is debt. Debt will never replace VC as the primary source of funding for a company – nor should it. But they can be used together to strengthen founders' positions.

## "Debt Be Not Proud"

The winter of 2023, as I was finishing this book, was not an ideal time for raising equity. Noted Rob Winkelmann, founder and CEO of Credo 180°, "It's a bear market, and valuations are down. Now is not a time that a lot of people want to raise equity."

He also noted that his firm, Credo 180°, which advises businesses at all stages on debt financing, has been busier in the past 18 months – roughly June 2021 through early 2023 – than ever. "Everybody's looking at debt," Rob says, and he predicts it will remain that way until the equity markets pick up and valuations improve. "If you qualify for debt, and debt is structured appropriately in the right amounts, it is a perfect solution to try and get through this period."

I've always been an advocate for taking on debt when you can raise equity but choose not to, and also for the idea that they should be used together. Now there may be a case to be made for not looking at equity right now and for relying more heavily and exclusively on venture debt – albeit as a temporary solution.

This comes with the caveats that you need to be a good prospect for a lender, that debt needs to make sense for your company, and that you should be looking at using it for the traditional reasons that debt makes sense – that it can extend your runway, help you achieve the milestones necessary to get to the next stage, or to hire critical personnel.

Rob asked the rhetorical question, "Will lenders do debt without some equity because they know how hard it is to raise equity?" I think the other question suggested by current conditions is, "Will companies that haven't looked at debt before consider it now?"

I believe the answer is yes. It's likely that many of these companies are perfectly good candidates for debt but didn't know about it or understand it. If the utility and flexibility of debt becomes better known, that will be a good thing not just for lenders like Runway Growth but for entrepreneurs/founders and equity investors.

We are seeing changes in the demographics of the Valley among both VCs and founders. Groups not typically represented are being seen in greater numbers. I'm not going to pretend that all sins of the past are made up for, but there is no going backward.

The changes have been slow to come but they are taking root and I'm confident that going forward we will continue to see more businesses founded, funded, and run by people who have not had access to either the education or resources that they historically lacked.

Among the most profound changes has been the amounts of money at play. Seed is the new Series A. Late-stage rounds grew to be the size of an IPO with none of the risks and required selling to only a few investors. As a result, many companies are delaying or rethinking going public. Why give up autonomy, go through an excruciating amount of work and incur considerable cost, and subject themselves to different requirements and a new set of risks?

More than one person has asked if there has been too much money available, and if that makes both investors and founders almost cavalier about risk and failure. Could there be changes to how funding works? Yes, but I don't think the money in and of itself in the innovation ecosystem is an issue.

There have been enormous amounts of money made available, but there is almost an endless amount of innovation to be funded. The incredibly positive overall returns that have been generated, not merely in financial terms, speak for themselves. This is productive money that is both generating return and improving society, making the economy more efficient and making the world a better place.

The sources of money, as well as greed and outsized competitiveness, are more likely culprits. In recent times an insane amount of equity capital, much of it from sources outside traditional VC (hedge funds, sovereign wealth funds, mutual funds, large corporations), has focused on startups and led to a diminution of proper corporate governance, including the rise of the dual-share classes, where the entrepreneur completely controls the company.

Founders ended up without the kind of guardrails they should have had. We saw this happen at both Uber and WeWork, and it's even true at Meta, where Mark Zuckerberg has been free to pursue his dream of the metaverse, despite controversy both from within the company and from shareholders.

People might wonder why I am writing about vast sums of money being available given that as I was writing this book Silicon Valley was going through one of its "periodic purges."

To young people, some of the shakeouts we are seeing in the Valley are scary indeed. To someone who was a VC during the severe tech downturn of 2000 to 2002 and again during the more widespread 2007–2009 financial crisis, I say with confidence that this is yet another cycle and that there is still sufficient money out there, both in the VC world and among the debt community, to help the most deserving companies.

Yes, some companies will fail, but it's a healthy culling required to weed out the top-of-cycle excess and allow the most promising companies to prosper. As in previous downturns, this era will spur a new cycle of innovation. The people laid off today will start and/or work for new businesses that will be the innovation leaders of tomorrow.

I still feel tremendous optimism, and I know I am not alone. One of my favorite quotes for this book came from Pixlee GoTo's Kyle Wong. When speaking of the advantages of the startup world, he said, "It only takes one person to say yes – one investor who can give us the greenlight. If we were in the large corporate world, one person can say no and kill an innovative idea before it even has a chance to prove itself."

That to me speaks of the uniqueness and even the magic of the startup world. As Alec Wright said, "Even with the deck stacked against you, I think at the same time, there's never been a better time ever to be a founder of a tech company."

He points out that the cost of launching new software and products is a fraction today of what it was years ago, thanks to available infrastructure and the development of no-code platforms, turnkey SaaS systems and platforms, and the sheer amount of capital and support infrastructure available today. Indeed, the shift from hardware to software, services, and apps has been one of the most profound shifts, changing both the speed and the cost of innovation.

Alec echoes Kyle's point about the special nature of start-ups. "The thing that attracts me to it, the thing that I love most about it, and the thing that creates the most challenge around the learning curve of being a first-time founder, is that launching and founding a venture-backed business is completely different than launching a small- and medium-size business," he continues. "It's different than running or working in a massive company. There's a different playbook and a different language; there's a different gravity in this world."

Luck can, and does, play a huge part in people's success. That's true of any business or any individual's life, but luck is seen as a tremendous force in the startup world because of scale – of money, of the potential to have an impact on the world, to change the way people live and work.

There are those who say that luck shows up when the hard work is done, and there is some truth to that. I've both worked hard and been lucky, and I think everyone interviewed for this book would say the same about themselves. The nature of luck is that it is capricious and unfair. There's nothing wrong with being lucky. Savor it – but remember that luck is no more a strategy than hope is, and luck is not a substitute for hard work.

I feel fortunate – perhaps another way of saying lucky – to play a part in helping founders see their dreams come true, in helping companies succeed, and for being a part of probably the greatest growth engine of technological and societal change across the globe.

If this book has helped any of you along your way, I'll feel that much more fortunate, and I wish you all good luck along the way.

David Spreng

# Appendix

## Glossary

**409A valuation:**  An independent appraisal of the fair market value (FMV) of a private company's common stock (the stock reserved mainly for founders and employees). The 409A valuation is used to establish the exercise price for options granted to employees. The name of the valuation refers to section 409A of the IRS's internal revenue code (IRC). Performing regular 409A valuations provides protection to employees that they will not be subject to potential taxes for "cheap stock" gains in the event of a successful exit.[1]

**Accelerator:**  A program that gives developing companies access to mentorship, investors, and other support that help them become stable, self-sufficient businesses.[2] Accelerators are for businesses that have developed a minimum viable product (MVP) and want to progress quickly into ramping revenues.

**Acquihire:**  When a company buys another company primarily for its employees instead of acquiring the company for its products or services, or its financial assets.

**Angel investor:**  Also known as a private investor, seed investor, or angel funder, an angel investor is a high-net-worth individual who provides financial backing for small startups or entrepreneurs, typically in exchange for ownership equity in the company. The funds that angel investors provide may be a one-time investment to help the business get off the ground or an ongoing injection to support and carry the company through its difficult early stages.

---

[1] https://carta.com/blog/what-is-a-409a-valuation/.
[2] https://www.mybusinessgrowth.online/business-acceleration-program.

**ARR:**   The acronym for annual recurring revenue, a key metric used by SaaS or subscription businesses that have term subscription agreements, meaning there is a defined contract length. It is defined as the value of the contracted recurring revenue components of your term subscriptions normalized to a one-year period. Typically, it will include only contractually committed, fixed subscription fees. Since one-time fees are by definition nonrecurring, they are almost always excluded from ARR calculations.

**Asset-based lending:**   The business of loaning money in an agreement that is secured by collateral. An asset-based loan or line of credit may be secured by inventory, accounts receivable, equipment, or other property owned by the borrower. The asset-based lending industry serves business, not consumers.

**Basis points (also known as bps or "bips"):**   A unit of measure used in finance to describe the percentage change in the value of financial instruments or the rate change in an index or other benchmark. One basis point is equivalent to 0.01% (1/100th of a percent) or 0.0001 in decimal form. Likewise, a fractional basis point such as 1.5 basis points is equivalent to 0.015% or 0.00015 in decimal form. In most cases, basis points refer to changes in interest rates and bond yields.

**Bootstrapping:**   Describes a situation in which an entrepreneur starts a company with little capital, relying on money other than outside investments. An individual is said to be bootstrapping when they attempt to found and build a company from personal finances or the operating revenues of the new company.

**Book runner:**   The primary underwriter or lead coordinator in the issuance of new equity, debt, or securities instruments. The book runner (or bookrunner) is the lead underwriting firm that runs or is in charge of the books in investment banking.

**Bulge-bracket investment bank:**   A catchall term for the most profitable multinational investment banks in the world, whose banking clients are normally large institutions, corporations, and governments. Then there are boutique banks – smaller, younger banks that specialize in certain areas of investment banking and handle smaller deals.

**Business-to-business (B2B or B-to-B):**  A form of transaction between businesses, such as one involving a manufacturer and wholesaler, or a wholesaler and a retailer. Business-to-business refers to business that is conducted between companies rather than between a company and individual consumer. Business-to-business stands in contrast to business-to-consumer (B2C) and business-to-government (B2G) transactions.

**Business-to-consumer (B2C):**  The process of selling products and services directly between a business and consumers who are the end users of its products or services. Most companies that sell directly to consumers can be referred to as B2C companies.

**Capitalization (cap) table:**  A spreadsheet or table that shows the equity capitalization for a company. A capitalization table is most commonly utilized for startups and early-stage businesses but all types of companies may use it as well. In general, the capitalization table is an intricate breakdown of a company's shareholders' equity. Cap tables often include all of a company's equity ownership capital, such as common equity shares, preferred equity shares, warrants, and convertible equity.

**Churn rate:**  Also known as the rate of attrition or customer churn, the churn rate is the rate at which customers stop doing business with an entity. It is most commonly expressed as the percentage of service subscribers who discontinue their subscriptions within a given time period. It is also the rate at which employees leave their jobs within a certain period. For a company to expand its clientele, its growth rate (measured by the number of new customers) must exceed its churn rate.

**Compliance certificate:**  A certificate accompanying the financial statements given by a borrower to a lender under the terms of a loan agreement. The form of certificate is usually attached to the loan agreement as a schedule. Typically, the certificate:

- Sets out details of financial covenants contained in the loan agreement as at a certain date or for a certain period.
- States whether the borrower has complied with the financial covenants.

The certificate may also confirm that no event of default has occurred, or, if an event of default *has* occurred, the nature of that default and any steps being taken to remedy it.

**Convertible notes:**    Debt that converts into equity. In the context of a seed financing, the debt typically automatically converts into shares of preferred stock upon the closing of a Series A round of financing. In other words, investors loan money to a startup as its first round of funding; and then rather than get their money back with interest, the investors receive shares of preferred stock as part of the startup's initial preferred stock financing, based on the terms of the note.[3]

**Covenant:**    In its broadest sense, a promise, agreement, or contract between two parties. As part of the covenant, the two parties agree that certain activities will or will not be carried out. Covenants in finance most often relate to terms in a financial contract.

**Dilution:**    Occurs when a company issues new shares that result in a decrease in existing stockholders' ownership percentage of that company. Stock dilution can also occur when holders of stock options, such as company employees, exercise their options. When the number of shares outstanding increases, each existing stockholder owns a smaller, or diluted, percentage of the company, making each share less valuable.

**Distressed lending:**    The process of investing capital in the debt of a financially distressed company, government, or public entity. A financially distressed company is one that has an unstable capital structure. This could mean that the company's debt load is too high or difficult to refinance, or the company can't meet restrictions on its current debt covenants.[4]

**Down round:**    A private company offering additional shares for sale at a lower price than what they had been sold for in the previous financing round. Simply put, more capital is needed and the company discovers that its valuation is lower than it was in the previous round of financing. This "discovery" forces them to sell their capital stock at a lower price per share.

---

[3]https://techcrunch.com/2012/04/07/convertible-note-seed-financings/.
[4]https://en.wikipedia.org/wiki/Distressed_lending.

**Dry powder:**   A slang term referring to money raised by VCs that hasn't yet been deployed. It is the amount of capital that VCs have available to invest in the future. Sometimes it is earmarked (notionally, not contractually) for specific existing portfolio companies. However, more often, it remains unallocated so that it can be used where most impactful over time as determined by the partners of the venture firm.

**Due diligence:**   An investigation, audit, or review performed to confirm facts or details of a matter under consideration. In the financial world, due diligence requires an examination of financial records before entering into a proposed transaction with another party.

**EBITDA:**   Earnings before interest, taxes, depreciation, and amortization – a standard accounting definition from the income statement. EBITDA is the best measure of profitability (used in determining valuation and evaluating debt service capacity) because it strips out the effects of a company's capital structure and tax situation.

**Enterprise value (EV):**   Measures a company's total value, often used as a more comprehensive alternative to equity market capitalization. EV includes in its calculation the market capitalization of a company as well as short-term and long-term debt and any cash or cash equivalents on the company's balance sheet.

**Enterprise value lending:**   Loans made based on enterprise value rather than cash flow or assets.

**Financial technology (better known as fintech):**   New tech that seeks to improve and automate the delivery and use of financial services. At its core, fintech is utilized to help companies, business owners, and consumers better manage their financial operations, processes, and lives by utilizing specialized software and algorithms that are used on computers and, increasingly, smartphones. *Fintech*, the word, is a combination of "financial technology."

**Growth lender:**   Provides funding to high-growth companies that traditional banks cannot or will not. Unlike traditional bank lending, this funding is available to businesses that do not have positive cash flows or significant assets to use as collateral.

**Impact investor:**   Someone who employs an investment strategy ("impact investing") that aims to generate specific beneficial social or environmental effects in addition to financial gains. Such investments may take the form of numerous asset classes and may result in many specific outcomes.

**Incubator:**   An organization engaged in the business of fostering early-stage companies through the different developmental phases until the companies have sufficient financial, human, and physical resources to function on their own.

**Investor (or pitch) deck:**   A brief presentation that gives potential investors an overview of a company's business plan, products, services, and growth traction.[5]

**Internal rate of return (IRR):**   A metric used in financial analysis to estimate the profitability of potential investments. IRR is a discount rate that makes the net present value (NPV) of all cash flows equal to zero in a discounted cash flow analysis.

**Lead director:**   Works with the chairman to ensure that the board is able to carry out its responsibilities effectively and independently of both management and the company's controlling shareholders.[6]

**Lead investor (or lead):**   The first or largest or most influential investor to commit to a given round of funding and who agrees to set the terms for any other investors who participate in the financing. This is called "leading the round." The lead investor normally makes the largest investment in the round and commonly takes a board seat as part of the deal.[7]

**Lead underwriter:**   An investment bank that has the primary directive of organizing an initial public stock offering (IPO) or a secondary offering for public companies. A lead underwriter usually works with other investment banks to establish an underwriter syndicate and is responsible for assessing the company's financials and current market conditions to arrive at the initial value and number of shares to be sold.

---

[5]https://visme.co/blog/what-is-a-pitch-deck/.
[6]https://www.financierworldwide.com/the-role-of-the-lead-director.
[7]https://www.holloway.com/g/venture-capital/sections/rounds.

**Limited partnership (LP):**    Not to be confused with a limited liability partnership (LLP), a limited partnership is a partnership made up of two or more partners. The general partner oversees and runs the business while limited partners do not participate in managing the business. However, the general partner of an LP has unlimited liability for any obligations of the partnership, and any limited partners have limited liability up to the amount of their investment.

**Loan-to-own:**    A lending strategy in which the lender anticipates that the borrower will default on the loan, allowing the lender to foreclose and therefore own the business or assets.

**Monthly recurring revenue (MRR):**    An important metric for subscription-based businesses, MRR is calculated by multiplying the total number of paying users by the average monthly revenue per user.

**Multiple on invested capital (MOIC):**    A metric used to describe the value or performance of an investment relative to its initial cost, commonly used within private markets. Unlike the internal rate of return (IRR), MOIC does not measure the profitability of an investment over time. It does not take into account the time value of money. MOIC equals the value of an investment divided by the cost of the investment. Also known as cash-on-cash return.

**Minimum viable product (MVP):**    A version of a product with just enough features to be usable by early customers, who can then provide feedback for future product development.[8]

**Nondilutive:**    Usually, a type of financing for a business where shares are not issued in return for the investment. Existing investors' ownership in the company is not diluted by issuing new shares.

**Observers:**    Board observers are startup board participants who don't possess voting rights.

**Outsourcing:**    The business practice of hiring a party outside a company to perform services or create goods that were traditionally performed in-house by the company's own employees and staff. Outsourcing is a practice usually undertaken by companies to manage costs. It is often done not to cut costs but to make costs variable versus fixed.

---

[8]https://en.wikipedia.org/wiki/Minimum_viable_product.

**Placement agent:**   A company that specializes in finding investors for an offering of debt or equity. Placement agents are typically compensated as a percentage of the capital they raise. Sometimes a venture-backed company will hire a placement agent to raise capital to allow the management team to remain focused on building the company.

**Price-to-earnings or PE ratio:**   The ratio for valuing a company that measures its current share price relative to its earnings per share (EPS). The price-to-earnings ratio is also sometimes known as the price multiple or the earnings multiple. PE ratios are used by investors and analysts to determine the relative value of a company's shares in an apples-to-apples comparison. They can also be used to compare a company against its own historical record or to compare aggregate markets against one another or over time.

**Private equity (PE):**   Investment firms that buy and manage companies before selling them. Private equity firms operate investment funds on behalf of institutional and accredited investors. Private equity funds may acquire private companies or public ones in their entirety, or invest in such buyouts as part of a consortium. They typically do not hold stakes in companies that remain listed on a stock exchange. Private equity is often grouped with venture capital and hedge funds as an alternative investment. Investors in this asset class are usually required to commit significant capital for years, which is why access to such investments is limited to institutions and individuals with high net worth.

**Recapitalization (recap):**   The process of restructuring a company's debt and equity mixture, often to stabilize a company's capital structure. The process mainly involves the exchange of one form of financing for another, such as removing preferred shares from the company's capital structure and replacing them with bonds.

**Recurring revenue loan:**   A loan that is made available and sized on the basis of the revenue stream of a company and the recurring nature of that revenue stream. The borrower of a recurring revenue loan is expected to show a book of expected revenues usually arising from contracts with customers. This has made the product popular in the context of expanding software businesses and other businesses that can show strong committed revenue streams from customer contracts but lack the EBITDA needed for a cashflow loan.[9] Not to be confused with revenue-based financing (see below).

**Recycle funds:** Fund managers (known as general partners or GPs) who want to put more of the raised fund's capital to work can do so through a process known as "recycling." This is where GPs reinvest some of the returns from early exits back into the fund for new investments (instead of distributing the returns to the fund's limited partners or LPs). This allows the fund to take a few "extra shots on goal" and can positively impact overall returns.[10]

**Revenue-based financing:** A method of raising capital for a business from investors who receive a percentage of the enterprise's ongoing gross revenues in exchange for their investment. In a revenue-based financing investment, investors receive a regular share of the business's revenue until a predetermined amount has been paid. Typically, this predetermined amount is a multiple of the principal investment and usually ranges between 1.5 and 5 times the original amount invested. *Not to be confused with recurring revenue loans (see above).*

**Revesting shares:** A concept applied to founder equities. Although they own the shares of their company at the outset, the company has the option to buy back their shares if they decide to leave or are terminated for cause. The percentage of shares the company can buy back in such an eventuality decreases as the duration of the founders' stay with the company increases. It's kind of a reverse vesting scenario where the longer a founder stays with the company, the fewer the shares the company can buy back from them if they decide to quit.[11]

**Runway:** A cash runway is an estimate of how long a business can continue to operate before it runs out of cash. Business owners can use a cash runway to understand how much time they

---

[9]https://www.mofo.com/resources/insights/211109-rise-recurring-revenue-loans-europe.
[10]https://learn.angellist.com/articles/recycling.
[11]https://thebusinessprofessor.com/en_US/business-transactions/reverse-vesting-definition.

have before needing to secure additional funding. This is especially important for early-stage businesses that are just starting out and may not have access to traditional forms of financing.[12] Cash runway = Cash balance/Burn rate.

**SAFE (Simple Agreement for Future Equity) agreement:** Developed by Y Combinator in 2013 to help young startup companies raise capital quickly and easily. Since then, this template has been a staple in the tech startup community. A SAFE is frequently used in early-stage rounds (pre-seed and seed) as an alternative to a convertible note or a priced round.

**Sand Hill Road:** A 5.6-mile stretch of roadway that cuts through Palo Alto, Menlo Park, and Woodside, CA. This proximity to Silicon Valley made it the perfect location for venture capital firms to establish or expand their presence and build relationships with promising and successful companies in the area.[13] The road has become a metonym for that industry.

**Secondary direct investment:** The buying and selling of an investor's ownership in a privately held, venture capital, or private equity–backed company.[14]

**Silicon Valley:** A region in the south San Francisco Bay Area. The name was first adopted in the early 1970s because of the region's association with the silicon transistor, which is used in all modern microprocessors. The area is notable for the vast number of technology companies that are headquartered there. As such, Silicon Valley is a global hub for technological innovation, where hundreds of companies call it home. It is also known for being a center for innovation, entrepreneurial spirit, and a lifestyle founded on technologically based wealth.

**Sweeping cash:** When a lender, following a default, takes control of a borrower's bank account(s) and moves (sweeps) the cash from the borrower's account to the lender's account. Nearly all venture debt loans will include a provision that allows the lender, in the event of a borrower default, to take control of the borrower's cash accounts. From there, the lender can sweep the cash by instructing the bank to wire the funds elsewhere.

---

[12]https://www.causal.app/define/cash-runway-e.
[13]https://www.builtinsf.com/2020/04/01/sand-hill-road.
[14]https://extopartners.com/blog/what-is-a-direct-secondary-fund/.

**Syndicate:**   A temporary alliance of businesses that join together to manage a large transaction that would be difficult, or impossible, to effect individually. Syndication makes it easy for companies to pool their resources and share risks, as when a group of investment banks works together to bring a new issue of securities to the market. There are different types of syndicates, such as underwriting syndicates, banking syndicates, and insurance syndicates.

**Term loan:**   Term loans have a fixed term, usually between one and ten years. The interest rate is most often variable and floats with a spread above a base of Prime, SOFR or a similar benchmark rate. Term loans are often used for small business and midsized corporate loans. The ability to repay over a long period of time is attractive for new or expanding enterprises, as the assumption is that they will increase their profit over time. Term loans are a good way of quickly increasing capital.

**Unicorn:**   A privately held company with a value of more than $1 billion. The term was made popular by venture capitalist Aileen Lee. Unicorns are extremely rare and require innovation. Because of their sheer size, unicorn investors tend to be private investors or venture capitalists, which means the chance to invest in a unicorn is often out of the reach of retail investors. Although it isn't necessary, many unicorns work their way to going public.

**Venture backed:**   A company that has raised capital from VCs.

**Venture capital (VC):**   A form of private equity and a type of financing that investors provide to startup companies and small businesses that are believed to have long-term growth potential.

**Venture capitalist (VC):**   An investor that provides capital to companies with high growth potential in exchange for an equity stake. VCs typically invest in companies that are not yet profitable. The use of proceeds is typically to fund losses in pursuit of growth.

**Venture debt:**   A form of minimally dilutive funding for high-growth venture-backed companies. Typically structured as a three-to-five-year term loan, proceeds are used to fund working capital, growth initiatives, acquisitions, or to refinance existing debt. It can be a replacement for or a complement to equity financing. When utilized properly, venture debt can help a business grow without its founders having to incur unnecessary dilution or give away control of their company. And unlike traditional bank lending, it is available to businesses that do not have positive cash flows or significant assets to use as collateral.

**Warrants:**    A derivative that gives the right, but not the obligation, to buy or sell a security – most commonly an equity – at a certain price before expiration. The price at which the underlying security can be bought or sold is referred to as the exercise price or strike price. Warrants are commonly granted to providers of venture debt to provide lenders with equity upside (a "kicker"). Warrants that give the right to buy a security are known as call warrants; those that give the right to sell a security are known as put warrants.

**Workout agreement:**    A contract mutually agreed to between a lender and borrower to renegotiate the terms on a loan that is in default. Generally, the workout includes waiving any existing defaults and restructuring the loan's terms and covenants. A workout agreement is only possible if it serves the interests of both the borrower and the lender.

**Wipeout:**    A financing round in which the price and structure greatly penalizes existing investors who chose not to participate. The ownership positions of investors that chose not to participate are generally "wiped out" such that they have no or little value.

**Yet to be profitable:**    Companies that are still growing but aren't making money. They are often on a "path to profitability" and their business model (margins, etc.) supports achieving profitability with additional scale (revenue growth).

## Recommended Reading, Listening, and Viewing

As I mentioned earlier in the book, there are scores of fine books on all the subjects touched on here, as well as on other subjects on which we've barely scratched the surface, most notably leadership and management. A big plus is that now you can listen to books: take advantage of your limited downtime to either read or listen to a few good ones.

In addition to the books cited in the text, I recommend *The Power Law*, by Sebastian Malachy, an in-depth book on all things

VC-related. Clint D. Korver's book *Ethics for the Real World* is a practical but principled book about doing the right thing. Executive coach Marshall Goldsmith has written a number of fine books, and I particularly like *What Got You Here Won't Get You There*. It's very apt for the startup world, where having a great idea won't guarantee you success as an executive.

As far as biographies of personal heroes, we each have those people we admire and wish we could emulate (though we fear we have no chance of doing so). Despite their reminders of my own shortcomings, I especially enjoy reading about entrepreneurs and their stories of success. Three books I especially like are *Shoe Dog* by Nike founder Phil Knight, *Market Mover: Lessons from a Decade of Change at Nasdaq* by the exchange's former CEO (and Runway board member) Robert Greifeld, and *Quench Your Own Thirst* by Sam Adams brewer and founder Jim Koch.

When I was a fledgling investment banker, *Wall Street* was about the only Hollywood depiction of our field, and to say we didn't come off so great is an understatement. *Something Ventured* is a 2011 documentary about the birth of venture capital in the mid-twentieth century. It's more historical than instructive, but if you're a history buff, give it a watch. *The Social Network*, a fictionalized look at the founding of Facebook, produced in 2010, seems downright quaint now.

Options for more contemporary viewing include Mike Judge's brilliant, satirical, and extremely funny HBO series *Silicon Valley*, based in part on Judge's time as an engineer in the Valley in the 1980s. The series ran from 2014 to 2019, and was faithful both to modern times and Judge's earlier experiences, leading you to wonder if things truly ever change.

*Super Pumped* is a dramatized version of the founding of Uber. While it sometimes takes a sharp turn from actual events, it's worth a watch. And there's also 2022's *The Dropout*, a dramatized take on Elizabeth Holmes and now-defunct Theranos, and *WeCrashed*, about WeWork's founder Adam Neuman, his wife Rebekah, and the company's failed IPO attempt in 2019. There are also numerous documentaries on these people and companies, as well as countless other documentaries. They should all be viewed with a grain of salt, but many are still worth your time.

# FAQs

- **What is venture debt?**

    Venture debt is a form of minimally dilutive funding for high-growth venture-backed companies. Typically structured as a three-to-five-year term loan, proceeds are used to fund working capital, growth initiatives, and acquisitions, or to refinance existing debt. It can be a replacement for or a complement to equity financing. When utilized properly, venture debt can help a business grow without its founders having to incur unnecessary dilution or give away control of their company. And unlike traditional bank lending, it is available to businesses that do not have positive cash flows or significant assets to use as collateral.

- **What are the primary use cases?**
    - Fuel growth initiatives such as sales and marketing, product development, and/or business expansion.
    - Extend the cash runway to reach the next company milestone (and increase valuation ahead of the next equity raise).
    - Avoid a bridge round by borrowing between equity rounds.
    - Fund a large capital expenditure such as the purchase of equipment or an acquisition.
    - Used as an insurance policy to protect against unexpected business challenges or an economic downturn.
    - Refinance existing lenders that may be unable to scale or unwilling to take the time to understand your business.

- **What are the benefits of venture debt?**
    - **Debt is cheaper than equity.** Debt financing allows a company to raise capital without its founders, management, and early investors having to incur unnecessary equity dilution. If your business is successful (and growing), the value of that equity in the long run will likely far surpass the amount you would have paid with debt financing. In other words, the more profitable a company is or will be, the more costly it is to sacrifice equity. This makes debt a much lower cost of capital compared to equity financing, especially for high-growth companies.

- **Maintaining control of your business.** In many cases, equity financing requires giving up a seat on your board. This means there will be more opinions on how the business should be run. If you've been through multiple equity rounds and have added several new board members, you may no longer be the controlling voice. If you disagree with the approach of your fellow board members, they can overrule you and, in extreme cases, oust you from your own company. On the flipside, most venture debt lenders do not require a seat on the board. They generally don't get too involved in your business, as long as you're making on-time payments and meeting pre-agreed-on performance metrics and reporting obligations.
- **Quicker access to capital.** Raising equity financing can be time-consuming and cumbersome. Depending on the company, it can take six to nine months or more. However, raising debt financing can be done in as little as four to six weeks. The benefit here is not only quicker access to capital, but more time for you to spend where it matters most – growing your business. Debt saves you time both at the onset and throughout the duration of the loan.
- **When should you use venture debt?**
  - Alongside an equity round.
  - Between equity rounds (to prevent a bridge round, or to allow more time for progress to drive a higher equity valuation).
  - When you don't need it (as an insurance policy).
- **When should you not use venture debt?**
  - The company is on a downward or unpredictable trajectory (i.e., high burn rate, highly variable revenue stream, or revenue has stalled or declined) and it is difficult to predict with confidence the ability to service and repay the debt.
  - The use of the loan is unclear.
  - The business is shifting or pivoting its strategy.
  - Debt is being considered as a last resort for financing.

# Sample Term Sheet

September 23, 2015

Jens Ley
Chief Executive Officer
19/39, Inc.
19 North 39th Street
4th Floor
Palo Alto, CA

Dear Jens,

Runway Growth Credit Fund Inc. (the "Lender") is pleased to express its interest in providing up to $30,000,000 in growth capital financing (the "Committed Loan Amount") to 19/39, Inc. (the "Borrower") on the terms and conditions detailed below:

| | |
|---|---|
| Description: | Senior Secured Term Loan (the "Loan"). |
| Loan Amount: | Up to $30,000,000 consisting of: |
| | Tranche I: $20,000,000 available at closing (the "Initial Closing"). |
| | Tranche II: $10,000,000 available upon the Borrower achieving $70,000,000 or more of fiscal year 2023 GAAP revenue (the "Tranche II Availability Milestone"). Tranche II may be drawn at any point within the six-month period immediately following achievement of the Tranche II Availability Milestone assuming Borrower's continued compliance with all covenants. |
| Purpose: | General corporate purposes including retirement of existing debt, but excluding shareholder dividends, distributions, and/or share repurchases. |

| | |
|---|---|
| Collateral: | Borrower shall grant Lender a first-position lien and perfected security interest in all assets of Borrower and its subsidiaries, including intellectual property, now existing or hereafter acquired. |
| | Borrower will be required to provide a Deposit Account Control Agreement(s) covering all Borrower's deposit, saving, and securities accounts. |
| Interest Rate: | The greater of (i) 7.00% + the three-month CME term secured overnight financing rate ("SOFR"), subject to a SOFR floor equal to SOFR at Initial Closing, or (ii) 10.50%. Interest will be payable in cash, monthly in arrears, on the 15th of each month (the "Payment Date"), beginning on the next Payment Date after Initial Closing. |
| Final Payment Fee: | In conjunction with and in addition to the final principal installment with respect to the Loan, the Borrower will pay a Final Payment Fee of 3.00% of the Committed Loan Amount. |
| Loan Maturity: | 48 months. |
| Interest-Only Period: | 24 months. |
| Amortization Period: | Beginning on month 25 and each month thereafter, Borrower will repay 1/24th of the outstanding Loan amount. Any months in which the Loan does not amortize shall be deemed the "Interest-Only Period." |
| Commitment Fee: | Borrower will pay a Commitment Fee equal to 1.00% of the Committed Loan Amount at the Initial Closing. |
| Prepayment Fees: | Months 1–12: 3.00% of the amount prepaid. Months 13–24: 2.00% of the amount prepaid. Months 25–36: 1.00% of the amount prepaid. Thereafter: None. |

| | |
|---|---|
| Success Fee: | Upon a change in control or liquidity event, Borrower shall pay to Lender a one-time, non-refundable Success Fee equal to 3.00% of the Committed Loan Amount. |
| Application Fee: | To commence due diligence, Borrower will pay an Application Fee of $50,000 upon the execution of this Term Sheet. Any amount available after Diligence Expenses shall be credited against the Commitment Fee. |

Financial Covenants of the Borrower:

i. Borrower shall achieve no less than 85% of planned fiscal year 2023 GAAP revenue per the Lender-approved operating plan, tested quarterly. Revenue levels to be reestablished in subsequent years using Board-approved operating plans.

ii. Borrower shall maintain at all times a cash balance sufficient to cover the subsequent six (6) months of negative cash flow including capex and debt service.

Equity Investment Requirement:

If at any point Borrower's cash balance does not meet or exceed $5,000,000, Borrower shall be required to secure at least $10,000,000 of incremental capital in the form of equity or convertible notes, which must be subordinated to Lender.

Reporting Requirements:

The Loan documents will provide for customary reporting, including:

- Monthly unaudited financial statements; AR and AP aging reports; and KPI, operating, and performance reporting.
- Quarterly board books.
- Annual audited financial statements; 409A valuations; and operating budget.
- Other items as the Lender may reasonably request and is customary for loans of this type.

| | |
|---|---|
| Events of Default: | Failure to make any payments when due, incurrence of additional indebtedness (unless otherwise approved by and on terms satisfactory to Lender), default on any other material debt or contract of the Borrower, failure to maintain covenants of the Borrower, and other events of default customary for a loan of this type, including a material adverse change. |
| Conditions Precedent to Funding: | • Retirement of all existing debt.<br>• Satisfactory completion of due diligence by Lender in its sole discretion (including, but not limited to, further analysis of churn, revenue concentrations, and competition).<br>• Approval of Lender's Investment Committee in its sole discretion.<br>• All necessary approvals by Borrower to enter into the transaction.<br>• A material adverse change has not occurred prior to Closing.<br>• Other conditions customary for loans of this type. |
| Document Preparation Fees and Expenses: | Borrower shall pay the reasonable costs and expenses incurred by Lender in connection with the preparation, negotiation, and execution of the Loan Documents, including attorney's fees, filing fees, legal fees and other out-of-pocket expenses ("Legal Expenses"), and any reasonable out-of-pocket due diligence expenses, including but not limited to site visits, inspection of assets, travel, and database access fees ("Diligence Expenses"). If Borrower withdraws from the transaction described herein, then Borrower shall pay all Legal Expenses and Diligence Expenses incurred through the date on which Borrower communicated such decision to withdraw. |

If Lender withdraws from the transaction described herein, then Lender shall reimburse to Borrower the Application Fee less Diligence Expenses incurred, to the extent such a number is greater than $0 ("Borrower's Refund"), so long as Lender's decision to withdraw did not result from (i) a material change to the Borrower's financial profile, (ii) a material fact, misrepresentation, or omission discovered in confirmatory due diligence, or (iii) Borrower's request to materially deviate from the terms contemplated herein.

Managerial Assistance:    Lender is a Business Development Company ("BDC"), which is a class of investment company created by Congress in 1980 and regulated by the Investment Company Act of 1940. As a BDC, Lender is required to offer significant managerial assistance to companies in which it invests. Lender has extensive experience working with a wide range of companies to develop and implement strategy, raise capital, complete acquisitions, and generally grow businesses. At Borrower's request, Lender will make available, most likely subject to a modest fee, assistance with matters such as:

- Financial modeling
- Capital raising and structuring strategies
- Mergers and acquisitions
- General strategy
- Board member and management searches

Confidentiality:    The existence of this term sheet, its terms, and any discussions with Lender will be kept confidential by Borrower.

Exclusivity and Term Sheet Expiration Date:    Upon execution of this letter, Borrower hereby grants exclusivity to Lender through November 15, 2015, by which date Borrower and Lender mutually agree to use best efforts to complete the Initial Closing.

Acceptance of this letter and wiring of the Application Fee will constitute Borrower's instruction to commence Lender's due diligence and loan approval processes. If approved, Lender will commence preparation of definitive documentation, which shall supersede this letter. Except for (i) Borrower's obligation to pay the Legal Expenses and Diligence Expenses described above, (ii) Lender's obligation to pay the Borrower's Refund described above, and (iii) the confidentiality and exclusivity provisions, this letter and other communications and negotiations regarding the proposed Loan do not constitute an agreement or an offer and do not create any legal rights benefiting, or obligations binding on, either Borrower or Lender. If these basic terms and conditions are acceptable, please return an executed copy of this letter and the Application Fee to Lender by September 30, 2022.

The Application Fee should be wired to Pioneer Growth Credit Fund Inc. as follows:

| | |
|---|---|
| Bank: | US Bank |
| Address: | 1001 Federal Street, 3rd Floor, Boston, MA 02110 |
| ABA #: | 1234567 |
| Account #: | 987654321 |
| Account Name: | Pioneer Growth Credit Fund Inc. |
| Reference: | 19/39 |

We look forward to working with you and your team. Please contact us with any questions.

Sincerely,

David Crockett
Chief Executive Officer, Founder

Accepted and Agreed:

19/39, Inc.

By: _____
Name:
Title:
Date:

# Index